All Trivia

Logan Pearsall Smith

ALL TRIVIA

TRIVIA

MORE TRIVIA

AFTERTHOUGHTS

LAST WORDS

HARCOURT, BRACE AND COMPANY

NEW YORK

The Author

These pieces of moral prose have been written, dear Reader, by a large Carnivorous Mammal, belonging to that suborder of the Animal Kingdom which includes also the Orang-outang, the tusked Gorilla, the Baboon with his bright blue and scarlet bottom, and the gentle Chimpanzee.

List of Contents

TRIVIA

BOOK ONE

viii

BOOK TWO

MORE TRIVIA

AFTERTHOUGHTS

LAST WORDS   185

EPILOGUE   197

TRIVIA

Book One

'How blest my lot, in these sweet fields assign'd
Where Peace and Leisure soothe the tuneful mind.'

SCOTT, of Amwell, *Moral Eclogues* (1773).

PREFACE

'You must beware of thinking too much about Style,' said my kindly adviser, 'or you will become like those fastidious people who polish and polish away until there is nothing left.'

'Then there really are such people?' I asked eagerly. But the well-informed lady could give me no precise information about them.

I often hear of them in this tantalizing manner, and perhaps one of these days I shall have the luck to come across them.

TRIVIA

Happiness

Cricketers on village greens, hay-makers in the evening sunshine, small boats that sail before the wind—all these create in me the illusion of Happiness, as if a land of cloudless pleasure, a piece of the old Golden World, were hidden, not (as poets have fancied) in far seas or beyond inaccessible mountains, but here close at hand, if one could find it, in some valley. Certain grassy lanes seem to lead through the copses thither; the wild pigeons talk of it behind the woods.

Today

I woke this morning out of dreams into what we call Reality, into the daylight, the furniture of my familiar bedroom—in fact into the well-known, often-discussed, but, to my mind, as yet unexplained Universe.

Then I, who came out of the Eternal Silence and seem to be on my way thither, got up and spent the day as I usually spend it. I read, I pottered, I complained, and took exercise; and I sat punctually down to eat the cooked meals that appeared at regular intervals.

The Afternoon Post

The village Post Office, with its clock and letter-box, its postmistress lost in the heartless seductions of the Aristocracy and tales of coroneted woe, and the sallow-faced grocer watching from his window opposite, is the scene of a daily crisis in my life, when every afternoon my Soul and I walk there through the country lanes and ask that well-read young lady for my letters. We always expect good news and cheques; and then, of course, there is the magical Fortune which is coming, and word of it may reach me any day. What it is, this strange Felicity, or whence it shall arrive, I have no notion; but I hurry down in the morning to find the news on the breakfast table, open telegrams in delighted panic, and cry, 'Here it comes!' when in the night-silence I hear wheels approaching along the road. So, happy in the hope of Happiness, and not greatly concerned with any other interest or ambition, we live on in my quiet, ordered house; and so we shall live perhaps until the end. Is it merely the last great summons and revelation for which we are waiting?

The Busy Bees

Sitting for hours idle in the shade of an apple tree, near the garden-hives, and under the aerial thoroughfares of those honey-merchants,—sometimes when the noonday heat is loud with their minute industry, or when they fall in crowds out of the late sun to their night-long labours,—

I have sought instruction from the Bees, and tried to appropriate to myself the old industrious lesson.

And yet, hang it all, who by rights should be the teacher and who the learners? For those peevish, over-toiled, utilitarian insects, was there no lesson to be derived from the spectacle of Me? Gazing out at me with composite eyes from their joyless factories, might they not learn at last—could I not finally teach them—a wiser and more generous-hearted way to improve the shining hours?

The Wheat

The Vicar, whom I met once or twice in my walks about the fields, told me that he was glad that I was taking an interest in farming. Only my feeling about wheat, he said, puzzled him.

Now the feeling in regard to wheat which I had not been able to make clear to the Vicar, was simply one of amazement. Walking one day into a field that I had watched yellowing beyond the trees, I was dazzled by the glow and great expanse of gold. I bathed myself in the intense yellow under the intense blue sky; how it dimmed the oak trees and copses and all the rest of the English landscape! I had not remembered the glory of the Wheat; nor imagined in my reading that in a country so far from the Sun, there could be anything so rich, so prodigal, so reckless, as this opulence of ruddy gold, bursting out from the cracked earth as from some fiery vein beneath. I remembered how for thousands of years Wheat had been the staple of wealth, the hoarded wealth of famous cities and empires; I thought of the processes of corn-growing, the white oxen ploughing, the great barns, the winnowing fans, the mills with the splash of their wheels, or arms slow-turning in the wind; of cornfields at harvest-time, with shocks and sheaves in the glow of sunset, or under the sickle moon; what beauty it brought into the northern landscape, the antique, passionate, Biblical beauty of the South!

The Coming of Fate

When I seek out the sources of my thoughts, I find they had their beginning in fragile Chance; were born of little moments that shine for me curiously in the past. Slight the impulse that made me take this turning at the crossroads, trivial and fortuitous the meeting, and light as gossamer the thread that first knit me to my friend. These are full of wonder; more mysterious are the moments that must have brushed me evanescently with their wings and passed me by: when Fate beckoned and I did not see it, when new Life trembled for a second on the threshold; but the word was not spoken, the hand was not held out, and the Might-have-been shivered and vanished, dim as a dream, into the waste realms of non-existence.

So I never lose a sense of the whimsical and perilous charm of daily life, with its meetings and words and accidents. Why, today, perhaps, or next week, I may hear a voice, and, packing up my Gladstone bag, follow it to the ends of the world.

My Speech

'Ladies and Gentlemen,' I began—

The Vicar was in the chair; Mrs. La Mountain and her daughters sat facing us; and in the little schoolroom, with its maps and large Scripture prints, its blackboard with the day's sums still visible on it, were assembled the labourers of the village, the old family coachman and his wife, the one-eyed postman, and the gardeners and boys from the Hall. Having culled from the newspapers a few phrases, I had composed a speech which I delivered with a spirit and eloquence surprising even to myself. The Vicar cried, 'Hear, Hear!' the Vicar's wife pounded her umbrella with such emphasis, and the villagers cheered so heartily, that my heart was warmed. I began to feel the meaning of my own words; I beamed on the audience, felt that they were all my brothers, all wished well to the Republic; and it seemed to me an occasion to divulge my real ideas and hopes for the Commonwealth.

Brushing therefore to one side, and indeed quite forgetting my safe principles, I began to refashion and new-model the State. Most existing institutions were soon abolished; and then, on their ruins, I built up the bright walls and palaces of the City within me—the City I had read of in Plato. With enthusiasm, and, I flatter myself, with eloquence, I described it all—the Warriors, that race of golden youth bred from the State-ordered embraces of the brave and the fair; those philosophic Guardians, who, being ever accustomed to the highest and most extensive views, and thence contracting an habitual greatness, possessed the truest fortitude, looking down indeed with a kind of disregard on human life and death. And then, declaring that the pattern of this City was laid up in Heaven, I sat down, amid the cheers of the uncomprehending little audience.

And afterward, in my rides about the country, when I saw on walls and the doors of barns, among advertisements of sales, or regulations about birds' eggs or the movements of swine, little weather-beaten, old-looking notices on which it was stated that I would address the meeting, I remembered how the walls and towers of the City I built up in that little schoolroom had shone with no heavenly light in the eyes of the Vicar's party.

Stonehenge

There they sit for ever around the horizon of my mind, that Stonehenge circle of elderly disapproving Faces—Faces of the Uncles, and Schoolmasters and the Tutors who frowned on my youth.

In the bright center and sunlight I leap, I caper, I dance my dance; but when I look up, I see they are not deceived. For nothing ever placates them, nothing ever moves to a look of approval that ring of bleak, old, contemptuous Faces.

My Portrait

But after all I am no amoeba, no mere sack and stomach; I am capable of discourse, can ride a bicycle, look up trains in Bradshaw; in fact I am and calmly boast myself a Human Being—that Masterpiece of Nature, and noblest fruit of time;—I am a rational, polite, meat-eating Man.

What stellar collisions and conflagrations, what floods and slaughters and enormous efforts has it not cost the Universe to make me—of what astral periods and cosmic processes am I not the crown, the wonder?

Where, then, is the Esplanade or world-dominating Terrace for my sublime Statue; the landscape of palaces and triumphal arches for the background of my Portrait; stairs of marble, flung against the sunset, not too narrow and ignoble for me to pause with ample gesture on their balustraded flights?

Complex Questions

The Age, the Vicar would remark, was a serious one; Englishmen were met face to face with complex questions. But the questions that had an interest for me at that time, would no doubt have seemed to the Vicar, many of them, old and imaginary. I was too often occupied, I am afraid, with the complexities of my own thoughts; their odd travels and changes; their way of peopling English forests with wood-nymphs, or transforming English orchards—seen perhaps at dawn or in the late sunshine—into Hesperian gardens. Sometimes it was merely names that filled my mind: 'Magalat, Galgalat, Saraïm,' I syllabled to myself; were these the names of the Magi of the East; or Atos, Satos, Paratoras? What were the names of the nymphs

Actaeon surprised bathing with Diana? The names of the hounds that hunted to his death that rash intruder; Ladon, Harpyia, Laelaps, Oresitrophos, as some call them; or, as they are given in other authentic books, Boreas, Omelampus, Agreus, Aretusa, Gorgo?

Silvia Doria

Beyond the blue hills, within riding distance, there is a country of parks and beeches, with views of the faded, far-off sea. I remember in one of my rides coming on the place which was the scene of the pretty, old-fashioned story of Silvia Doria. Through the gates, with fine gate-posts, on which heraldic beasts, fierce and fastidious, were upholding coroneted shields, I could see, at the end of the avenue, the façade of the House, with its stone pilasters, and its balustrade on the steep roof.

More than one hundred years ago, in that Park, with its Italianized house, and level gardens adorned with statues and garden temples, there lived, they say, an old Lord with his two handsome sons. The old Lord had never ceased mourning for his Lady, though she had died a good many years before; there were no neighbours he visited, and few strangers came inside the great Park walls. One day in Spring, however, just when the apple trees had burst into blossom, the gilded gates were thrown open, and a London chariot with prancing horses drove up the Avenue. And in the chariot, smiling and gay, and indeed very beautiful in her dress of yellow silk, and her great Spanish hat with drooping feathers, sat Silvia Doria, come on a visit to her cousin, the old Lord.

It was her father who had sent her—that he might be more free, some said, to pursue his own wicked courses, —while others declared that he intended her to marry the old Lord's eldest son.

However this might be, Silvia Doria came like the Spring, like the sunlight, into the lonely place. Even the old Lord felt himself curiously happy when he heard her voice singing about the house; as for Henry and Francis, it was heaven for them just to walk by her side along the garden alleys.

And Silvia Doria, though hitherto she had been but cold toward the London gallants who had courted her, found, little by little, that her heart was not untouched.

But, in spite of her father, and her own girlish love of gold and rank, it was not for Henry that she cared, not for the old Lord, but for Francis, the younger son. Did Francis know of this? They were secretly lovers, the old scandal reported; and the scandal, it may be, had reached her father's ears.

For one day a coach with foaming horses, and the wicked face of an old man at its window, galloped up the avenue; and soon afterwards, when the coach drove away, Silvia Doria was sitting by the old man's side, sobbing bitterly.

And after she had gone, a long time, many of the eighteenth-century years went by without change. And then Henry, the elder son, was killed in hunting; and the old Lord dying a few years later, the titles and the great house and all the land and gold came to Francis, the younger son. But after his father's death he was but seldom there; having, as it seemed, no love for the place, and living for the most part abroad and alone, for he never married.

And again, many years went by. The trees grew taller and darker about the house; the yew hedges, unclipped now, hung their branches over the shadowy paths; ivy smothered the statues; and the plaster fell away in great patches from the discoloured garden temples.

But at last one day a chariot drove up to the gates; a footman pulled at the crazy bell, telling the gate-keeper that his mistress wished to visit the Park. So the gates creaked open, the chariot glittered up the avenue to the deserted place; and a lady stepped out, went into the garden, and walked among its moss-grown paths and statues. As the chariot drove out again, 'Tell your Lord,' the lady said, smiling, to the lodge-keeper, 'that Silvia Doria came back.'

Bligh House

To the West, in riding past the walls of Bligh, I remembered an incident in the well-known siege of that house, during the Civil Wars: How, among Waller's invading Roundhead troops, there happened to be a young scholar, a poet, and lover of the Muses, fighting for the cause, as he thought, of ancient Freedom, who, one day, when the siege was being more hotly urged, pressing forward and climbing a wall, suddenly found himself in a quiet garden by the house. And here, for a time forgetting, as it would seem, the battle, and heedless of the bullets that now and then flew past him like peevish wasps, the young Officer stayed, gathering roses—old-fashioned damask roses, streaked with red and white—which, for the sake of a Court Beauty, there besieged with her father, he carried to the house; falling, however, struck by a chance bullet, or shot perhaps by one of his own party. A few of the young Officer's verses, written in the stilted fashion of the time, and almost unreadable now, have been preserved. The lady's portrait hangs in the white drawing-room at Bligh; a simpering, faded figure, with ringlets and drop-pearls, and a dress of amber-coloured silk.

The Stars

Battling my way homeward one dark night against the wind and rain, a sudden gust, stronger than the others, drove me back into the shelter of a tree. But soon the Western sky broke open; the illumination of the Stars poured down from behind the dispersing clouds.

I was astonished at their brightness, to see how they filled the night with their lustre. So I went my way accompanied by them; Arcturus followed me, and becoming entangled in a leafy tree, shone by glimpses, and then emerged triumphant, Lord of the Western sky. Moving along the road in my waterproof and goloshes, my thoughts were among the Constellations. I too was one of the Princes of the starry Universe; in me also there was something that blazed, that glittered.

In Church

'For the Pen,' said the Vicar; and in the sententious pause which followed I felt that I would offer all the gold of Peru to avert or postpone the solemn, inevitable, and yet, as it seemed to me, perfectly appalling statement that 'the Pen is mightier than the Sword.'

Parsons

All the same I like Parsons; they think nobly of the Universe, and believe in Souls and Eternal Happiness. And some of them, I am told, believe in Angels—that there are Angels who guide our footsteps, and flit to and fro unseen on errands in the air about us.

The Sound of a Voice

As the thoughtful Baronet talked, as his voice went on sawing in my ears, all the light of desire, and of the sun, faded from the Earth; I saw the vast landscape of the world, dim, as in an eclipse; its populations eating their bread with tears, its rich men sitting listless in their palaces, and aged Kings crying, 'Vanity, Vanity, all is Vanity!' lugubriously, from their thrones.

What Happens

'Yes,' said Sir Thomas, speaking of a modern novel, 'it certainly does seem strange; but the novelist was right. Such things do happen.'

'But, my dear Sir,' I burst out, in the rudest manner, 'think what life is—just think what really happens! Why people suddenly swell up and turn dark purple; they hang themselves on meat-hooks; they are drowned in horse-ponds, are run over by butchers' carts, and are burnt alive—cooked like mutton chops!'

Luton

In a field of that distant, half-neglected farm, I found an avenue of great elms leading to nothing. But I could see where the wheat-bearing earth had been levelled into a terrace; and in one corner there were broken, overgrown gateposts, almost hid among great straggling trees of box.

This, then, was the place I had come to see. Here had stood the great house or palace, with its terraces, its princely gardens, and artificial waters; this field had once been the favourite resort of Eighteenth-century Fashion; the Duchesses and Beauties had driven hither in their gilt coaches, and the Beaux and Wits of that golden time of English Society. And although the house had long since vanished, and the plough had gone over its pleasant places, yet for a moment I seemed to see this fine company under the green and gold of that great avenue; seemed to hear the gossip of their uncharitable voices as they passed on into the shadows.

A Precaution

The folio gave at length philosophic consolations for all the misadventures said by the author to be inseparable from human existence—Poverty, Shipwrecks, Plagues, Famines, Flights of Locusts, Love-Deceptions, Inundations. Against these antique Disasters I armed my soul; and I thought it as well to prepare myself against the calamity called 'Cornutation,' or by other less learned names. How Philosophy taught that after all it was but a pain founded on conceit, a blow that hurt not; the reply of the Cynic philosopher to one who reproached him, 'Is it my fault or hers?' how Nevisanus advises the sufferer to ask himself if he have not offended; Jerome declared it impossible to prevent; how few or none are safe, and, as the Moon astronomically makes horns at the Earth, her Husband, so do the ladies in many countries, especially parts of Africa, punctually cornutate their consorts; how Caesar, Pompey, Augustus, Agamemnon, Menelaus, Marcus Aurelius, and many other great Kings and Princes had all worn Actaeon's badge; and how Philip turned it to a jest, Pertinax the Emperor made no reckoning of it; Erasmus declared it was best winked at, there being no remedy but patience, *Dies dolorem minuit;* Time, Age must mend it; and how, according to the authorities, bars, bolts, oaken doors, and towers of brass, are all in vain. 'She is a woman,' as the old Pedant wrote to a fellow Philosopher. . . .

The Great Work

Sitting, pen in hand, alone in the stillness of the library, with flies droning behind the sunny blinds, I considered in my thoughts what should be the subject of my great Work. Should I complain against the mutability of Fortune, and impugn Fate and the Stars; or should I reprehend the never-satisfied heart of querulous Man, drawing elegant contrasts between the unsullied snow of mountains, the serene shining of the planets, and our hot, feverish lives and foolish repinings? Or should I confine myself to denouncing, like Juvenal or Jeremiah, contemporary Vices, crying 'Fie!' on the Age with Hamlet, inexorably unmasking its hypocrisies, and riddling through and through its too-comfortable Optimisms?

Or with Job, should I question the Universe, and puzzle my sad brains about Life—the meaning of Life on this apple-shaped Planet?

My Mission

But when in modern books, reviews, and thoughtful magazines I read about the Needs of the Age, its Complex Questions, its Dismays, Doubts, and Spiritual Agonies, I feel an impulse to go out and comfort that bewildered Epoch, to wipe away its tears, still its cries, and speak edifying words of Consolation to it.

The Birds

But how can one toil at the great task with this hurry and tumult of birds just outside the open window? I hear the Thrush, and the Blackbird, that romantic liar; then the delicate cadence, the wiry descending scale of the Willow-wren, or the Blackcap's stave of mellow music. All these are familiar;—but what is that unknown voice, that thrilling note? I hurry out; the voice flees and I follow; and when I return and sit down again to my task, the Yellow-hammer trills his sleepy song in the noonday heat; the drone of the Greenfinch lulls me into dreamy meditations. Then suddenly from his tree-trunks and forest recesses comes the Green Woodpecker, to mock at me with an impudent voice full of liberty and laughter.

Why should all the birds of the air conspire against me? My concern is with our own sad Species, with lapsed and erroneous Humanity; not with that vagabond, inconsiderate, feather-headed race.

High Life

Although that immense Country House was empty and for sale, and I had got an order to view it, I needed all my courage to walk through the lordly gates, and up the avenue, and then to ring the resounding door-bell. And when I was ushered in, and the shutters were removed to illuminate those vast apartments, I sneaked through them, cursing the dishonest curiosity which had brought me into a place where I had no business. But I was treated with such deference, and so plainly regarded as a possible purchaser, that I soon began to give credence to the opulence imputed to me. From all the novels describing the mysterious and glittering life of the Great which I had read (and I have read thousands), there came to me the vision of my own existence in this Palace. I filled those vast halls with the glint of diamonds and stir of voices; I saw a vision of be-jewelled Duchesses sweeping in their tiaras down the splendid stairs.

But my Soul, in her swell of pride, soon outgrew these paltry limits. Oh, no! Never could I box up and house under that roof the Pomp, the Ostentation of which I was capable.

Then for one thing there was stabling for only forty horses; and this, of course, as I told them, would never do.

Empty Shells

They lie like empty sea-shells on the shores of Time, the old worlds which the spirit of man once built for his habi-tation, and then abandoned. Those little earth-centred, heaven-encrusted universes of the Greeks and Hebrews seem quaint enough to us, who have formed, thought by thought from within, the immense modern Cosmos in which we live—the great Creation of fire, planned in such immeasurable proportions, and moved by so pitiless a mechanism, that it sometimes appalls even its own creators.

The rush of the great rotating Sun daunts us; to think to the distance of the fixed stars cracks our brains.

But if the ephemeral Being who has imagined these eternal spheres and spaces must dwell almost as an alien in their icy vastness, yet what a splendour lights up for him and dazzles in those great halls! Anything less limitless would be now a prison; and he even dares to think beyond their boundaries, to surmise that he may one day outgrow this Mausoleum, and cast from him the material Creation as an integument too narrow for his insolent Mind.

At the Window

But then I drew up the curtain and looked out of the window. Yes, there it still was, the old External World, still apparently quite unaware of its own non-existence. I felt helpless, small-boyish before it: I couldn't pooh-pooh it away.

How It Happened

This vision or blur bubbled up, the Buddhists believe, from some unaccountable perturbation underneath the eternal serene of Nirvana; but the naked Thinkers of the Ganges look upon it as an optical delusion of Brahma's, when he slipped up and grew giddy a moment, and put his foot, so to speak, into this Misapprehension.

But we in the West believe that God created the world in the pure caprice of His superabundant Omnipotence;

that He clapped His hands when He finished it, and declared that it was very good, and just what He wanted.

Vertigo

Still, I don't like it; I can't approve of it; I have always thought it most regrettable that earnest and ethical Thinkers like ourselves should go scuttling through space in this undignified manner. Is it seemly that I, at my age, should be hurled with my books of reference, and bed-clothes, and hot-water bottle, across the sky at the unthinkable rate of nineteen miles a second? As I say, I don't at all like it. This universe of astronomical whirligigs makes me a little giddy.

That God should spend His eternity—which might be so much better employed—in spinning countless Solar Systems, and skylarking, like a great child, with tops and tee-totums—is not this a serious scandal? I wonder what all our circumgyrating Monotheists really do think of it?

The Evil Eye

Drawn by the unfelt wind in my little sail over the shallow estuary, I lay in my boat, lost in the dream of mere existence. The cool water glided through my trailing fingers; and leaning over, I watched the sands that slid beneath me, the weeds that languidly swayed with the boat's motion. I was the cool water, I was the gliding sand and the swaying weed, I was the sea and sky and sun, I was the whole vast Universe.

Then between my eyes and the sandy bottom a mirrored face looked up at me, floating on the smooth film of water over which I glided. At one look from that too familiar, and yet how sinister and goblin a face, my immeasurable Soul collapsed like a wrecked balloon; I shrank sadly back into my named personality, and sat there, shabby, hot, and very much bored with myself in my little boat.

Dissatisfaction

For one thing I hate spiders: I hate most kinds of insects. Their cold intelligence, their stereotyped, unremitting industry repel me. And I am not altogether happy about the future of the human race. When I think of the earth's refrigeration, and the ultimate collapse of our Solar System, I have grave misgivings. And all the books I have read and forgotten—the thought that my mind is really nothing but an empty sieve—often this, too, disconcerts me.

Self-control

Still I am not a pessimist, nor misanthrope, nor grumbler; I bear it all, the burden of Public Affairs, the immensity of Space, the brevity of Life, and the thought of the all-swallowing Grave;—all this I put up with without impatience. I accept the common lot. And if now and then for a moment it seems too much; if I get my feet wet, or have to wait too long for tea, and my Soul in these wanes of the moon cries out in French *C'est fini!* I always answer *Pazienza,* in Italian—*abbia la santa Pazienza!*

A Fancy

More than once, too, I have pleased myself with the notion that somewhere there is good Company which will like this small sententious Book—these Thoughts (if I may call them so) dipped up from that phantasmagoria or phosphorescence which, by some unexplained process of combustion, flickers over the large lump of gray soft matter in the bowl of my skull.

They

Their taste is exquisite; They live in Palladian houses, in a world of ivory and precious china, of old brickwork and stone pilasters. In white drawing-rooms I see Them, or on blue, bird-haunted lawns. They talk pleasantly of me, and Their eyes watch me. From the diminished, ridiculous picture of myself which the glass of the world gives me, I turn for comfort, for happiness to my image in the kindly mirror of those eyes.

Who are They? Where, in what paradise or palace, shall I ever find Them? I may walk all the streets, ring all the door-bells of the World, but I shall never find Them. Yet nothing has value for me save in the crown of Their approval; for Their coming—which will never be—I build and plant, and for Them alone I secretly write this Book, which They will never read.

In the Pulpit

The Vicar had certain literary tastes; in his youth he had written an *Ode to the Moon;* and he would speak of the difficulty he found in composing his sermons, week after week.

Now I felt that if I composed and preached sermons, I would by no means confine myself to the Vicar's threadbare subjects—I would preach the Wrath of God, and sound the Last Trump in the ears of my Hell-doomed congregation, cracking the heavens and collapsing the earth with the Thunders and eclipses of the great Day of Judgement. Then I might refresh them with high and incomprehensible Doctrines, beyond the reach of Reason—Predestination, Election, Reprobation, the Co-existences and Co-eternities of the undemonstrable Triad. And with what a holy vehemence would I exclaim and cry out against all forms of doctrinal Error—all the execrable hypotheses of the great Heresiarchs! Then there would be many ancient, learned and out of the way Iniquities to denounce, and splendid, neglected Virtues to inculcate—Apostolic Poverty, and Virginity, that precious jewel, that fair garland, so prized in Heaven, but so rare, they say, on earth.

For in the range of creeds and morals it is the highest peaks that shine for me with a certain splendour: Ah! It's towards those radiant Alps, that, if I were a Clergyman, I would lead my flocks to pasture.

Caravans

Always over the horizon of the Sahara move those soundless caravans of camels, swaying with their padded feet across the desert, I imagine, till in the remoteness of my mind they fade away, they vanish.

Human Ends

I really was impressed, as we paced up and down the avenue, by the Vicar's words, and weighty, weighed advice. He spoke of the various professions; mentioned contemporaries of his own who had achieved success: how one had a Seat in Parliament, might be given a Seat in the Cabinet when his party next came in; another was a Bishop with a Seat in the House of Lords; a third was a Barrister who was soon, it was said, to be raised to the Bench.

But in spite of my good intentions, my real wish to find, before it is too late, some career or other for myself (and the question is getting serious), I am far too much at the mercy of ludicrous images. Front Seats, Episcopal, Judicial, Parliamentary Benches—were all the ends then, I asked myself, of serious, middle-aged ambition only things to sit on?

Where?

I, who move and breathe and place one foot before the other, who watch the Moon wax and wane, and put off answering my letters, where shall I find the Bliss which dreams and blackbirds' voices promise, of which the waves whisper, and hand-organs in streets near Paddington faintly sing?

Does it dwell in some island of the South Seas, or far oasis among deserts and gaunt mountains; or only in those immortal gardens pictured by Chinese poets beyond the great, cold palaces of the Moon?

Lord Arden

'If I were Lord Arden,' said the Vicar, 'I would shut up that great House; it's too big—what can a young unmarried man . . . ?'

'If I were Lord Arden,' said the Vicar's wife (and Mrs. La Mountain's tone showed how much she disapproved of that young nobleman), 'if I were Lord Arden, I would live there, and do my duty to my tenants and neighbours.'

'If I were Lord Arden,' I said; but then it flashed vividly into my mind, suppose I really were this Sardanapalian young Lord? I quite forgot to whom I was talking; the Moralist within ceased to function; my memory echoed with the names of people who had been famous for their enormous pleasures; who had made loud their palaces with guilty revels, and with Pyramids, Obelisks, and half-acre

Tombs, had soothed their Pride. My mind kindled at the thought of these Audacities. 'If I were Lord Arden!' I shouted. . . .

The Starry Heaven

'But what are they really? What do they say they are?' the small young lady asked me. We were looking up at the Stars, which were quivering that night in splendid synods above the lawns and trees.

So I tried to explain some of the views that have been held about the stars. How people first of all had thought them mere candles set in the sky, to guide their own footsteps when the Sun was gone; till wise men, sitting on the Chaldean plains, and watching them with aged eyes, became impressed with the solemn view that those still and shining lights were the executioners of God's decrees, and irresistible instruments of His Wrath; and that they moved fatally among their celestial Houses to ordain and set out the fortunes and misfortunes of each race of newborn mortals. And so it was believed that every man or woman had, from the cradle, fighting for or against him or her, some great Star, Formalhaut, perhaps, Aldebaran, Altaïr: while great Heroes and Princes were more splendidly attended, and marched out to their forgotten battles with troops and armies of heavenly Constellations.

But this noble old view was not believed in now; the Stars were no longer regarded as malignant or beneficent Powers; and I explained how most serious people thought that somewhere—though just where they could not say—above the vault of Sky, was to be found the final home of earnest men and women, where, as a reward for their right views and conduct, they were to rejoice forever, wearing those diamonds of the starry night arranged in glorious crowns. This notion, however, had been disputed by Poets and Lovers: it was Love, according to these young astronomers, that moved the Sun and other Stars; the Constellations being heavenly palaces, where people who had adored each other were to meet and live always together after Death.

Then I spoke of the modern immensity of the unimaginable Skies. But suddenly the enormous meaning of my words rushed into my mind; I felt myself dwindling, falling through the blue. And yet, in that pause of acquiescence there thrilled through me no chill of death or nothingness, but the taste and joy of this Earth, this orchard-plot of earth, floating unknown, and very far away with her Moon and her meadows.

My Map

The 'Known World' I called the map, which I amused myself making for the children's schoolroom. It included France, England, Italy, Greece, and all the old shores of the Mediterranean; but the rest I marked 'Unknown'; sketching into the East the doubtful realms of Ninus and Semiramis; changing back Germany into the Hercynian Forest; and drawing pictures of the supposed inhabitants of these unexploited regions, Dog-Apes, Satyrs, Paiderasts and Bearded Women, Cimmerians involved in darkness, Amazons, and Headless Men. And all around the Map I coiled the coils, and curled the curling waves of the great Sea *Oceanus,* with the bursting cheeks of the four Winds, blowing from the four hinges of the World.

The Full Moon

And then one night, low above the trees, we saw the great, amorous, unabashed face of the full Moon. It was an exhibition that made me blush, feel that I had no right to be there. 'After all these millions of years, she ought to be ashamed of herself!' I cried.

The Snob

As I paced in fine company on that terrace, I felt chosen, exempt, and curiously happy. There was a glamour in the air, a something in the special flavour of that moment that was like the consciousness of Salvation, or the smell of ripe peaches, in August, on a sunny wall.

I know what you're going to call me, Reader; but I am not to be bullied by words. And, after all, why not let oneself be dazzled and enchanted? Are not illusions pleasant, and is this a world in which Romance hangs, so to speak, on every tree?

And how about your own life? Is that, then, so full of gaudy visions?

Companions

Dearest, prettiest, and sweetest of my retinue, who gather with delicate industry bits of silk and down from the bleak world to make the soft nest of my fatuous repose; who ever whisper honied words in my ear, or trip before me holding up deceiving mirrors—is it Hope, or is it not rather Vanity, that I love the best?

Desires

These exquisite and absurd fancies of mine—little curiosities, and greedinesses, and impulses to kiss and touch and snatch, and all the vanities and artless desires that nest and sing in my heart like birds in a bush—all these, we are now told, are an inheritance from our prehuman past, and were hatched long ago in very ancient swamps and forests. But what of that? I like to share in the dumb delights of birds and animals, to feel my life drawing its sap from roots deep in the soil of Nature. I am proud of those bright-eyed, furry, four-footed or scaly progenitors, and not at all ashamed of my cousins, the Apes and Peacocks and streaked Tigers.

Edification

'I must really improve my mind,' I tell myself, and once more begin to patch and repair that crazy structure. So I toil and toil on at the vain task of edification, though the wind tears off the tiles, the floors give way, the ceilings fall, strange birds build untidy nests in the rafters, and owls hoot and laugh in the tumbling chimneys.

The Rose

The old lady had always been proud of the great rose-tree in her garden, and was fond of telling how it had grown from a cutting she had brought years ago from Italy, when she was first married. She and her husband had been travelling back in their carriage from Naples (it was before the time of railways), and on a bad piece of road south of Siena they had broken down, and had been forced to pass the night in a little house by the roadside. The accommodation was wretched of course; she had spent a sleepless night, and rising early had stood, wrapped up, at her window, with the cool air blowing on her face, to watch the dawn. She could still, after all these years, remember the blue mountains with the bright moon above them, and how a far-off town on one of the peaks had gradually grown whiter and whiter, till the moon faded, the mountains were touched with the pink of the rising sun, and suddenly the town was lit as by an illumination, one window after another catching and reflecting the sun's beams, till at last the whole little city twinkled and sparkled up in the sky like a nest of stars.

Finding they would have to wait while their carriage was being repaired, they had driven that morning, in a local conveyance, up to the city on the mountain, where they had been told they would find better quarters; and there they had stayed two or three days. It was one of the miniature Italian cities with a high church, a pretentious piazza, a few narrow streets and little palaces, perched, all compact and complete, on the top of a mountain, within an enclosure of walls hardly larger than an English kitchen garden. But it was full of life and noise, echoing all day and all night with the sounds of feet and voices.

The Café of the simple inn where they stayed was the meeting-place of the notabilities of the little city; the *Sindaco,* the *avvocato,* the doctor, and a few others; and among them they noticed a beautiful, slim, talkative old man, with bright black eyes and snow-white hair—tall and straight and still with the figure of a youth, although the waiter told them with pride that the *Conte* was *molto vecchio*—would in fact be eighty in the following year. He was the last of his family, the waiter added—they had once been great and rich people—but he had no descendants; in fact the waiter mentioned with complacency, as if it were a story on which the locality prided itself, that the *Conte* had been unfortunate in love, and had never married.

The old gentleman, however, seemed cheerful enough; and it was plain that he took an interest in the strangers, and wished to make their acquaintance. This was soon effected by the friendly waiter; and after a little talk the old man invited them to visit his villa and garden which were just outside the walls of the town. So the next afternoon, when the sun began to descend, and they saw in glimpses through doorways and windows blue shadows spreading over the brown mountains, they went to pay their visit. It was not much of a place, a small, modernized, stucco villa, with a hot pebbly garden, and in it a stone basin with torpid goldfish, and a statue of Diana and her hounds against the wall. But what gave a glory to it was a gigantic rose-tree which clambered over the house, almost smothering the windows, and filling the air with the perfume of its sweetness. Yes, it was a fine rose, the *Conte* said proudly when they praised it, and he would tell the Signora about it. And as they sat there, drinking the wine he offered them, he alluded with the cheerful indifference of old age to his love affair, as though he took for granted that they had heard of it already.

'The lady lived across the valley there beyond that hill. I was a young man then, for it was many years ago. I used to ride over to see her; it was a long way, but I rode fast, for young men, as no doubt the Signora knows, are impatient. But the lady was not kind, she would keep me waiting, oh, for hours; and one day when I had waited very long I grew very angry, and as I walked up and down in the garden where she had told me she would see me, I broke one of her roses, broke a branch from it; and when I saw what I had done, I hid it inside my coat—so—; and when I came home I planted it, and the Signora sees how it has grown. If the Signora admires it, I must give her a cutting to plant also in her garden; I am told the English have beautiful gardens that are green, and not burnt with the sun like ours.'

The next day, when their mended carriage had come up to fetch them, and they were just starting to drive away from the inn, the *Conte's* old servant appeared with the rose-cutting neatly wrapped up, and the compliments and wishes for a *buon viaggio* from her master. The town collected to see them depart, and the children ran after their carriage through the gate of the little city. They heard a rush of feet behind them for a few moments, but soon they were far down toward the valley; the little town with all its noise and life was high above them on its mountain peak.

She had planted the rose at home, where it had grown and flourished in a wonderful manner; and every June the great mass of leaves and shoots still broke out into a passionate splendour of scent and crimson colour, as if in its root and fibres there still burnt angrily the passion of that Italian lover. Of course, said the old lady (who had outlived sixty generations of these roses), the old *Conte* must have died long ago; she had forgotten his name, and had even forgotten the name of the mountain city that she had stayed in, after first seeing it twinkling at dawn in the sky, like a nest of stars.

Tu Quoque Fontium—

Just to sit in the Sun, to apricot myself in its heat—this is one of my country recreations. And often I reflect what a thing after all it is, still to be alive and sitting here, above all the buried people of the world, in the kind and famous sunshine.

Beyond the orchard there is a place where the stream, hurrying out from under a bridge, makes for itself a quiet pool. A beech-tree upholds its green light over the blue water; and there, when I have grown weary of the sun, the great glaring undiscriminating Sun, I can shade myself and read my book. And listening to this water's pretty voices I invent for it exquisite epithets, calling it *silver-clean* or *moss-margined* or *nymph-frequented,* and trivially promise to place it among the learned fountains and pools of the world, making of it a cool green thought for English exiles in the glare of Eastern deserts.

The Spider

What shall I compare it to, this fantastic thing I call my Mind? To a waste-paper basket, to a sieve choked with sediment, or to a barrel full of floating froth and refuse?

No, what it is really most like is a spider's web, insecurely hung on leaves and twigs, quivering in every wind, and sprinkled with dewdrops and dead flies. And at its geometric centre, pondering for ever the Problem of Existence, sits motionless and spider-like the uncanny Soul.

The Age

Again, as the train drew out of the station, the old gentleman pulled out of his pocket his great shining watch; and for the fifth, or as it seemed to me, the five hundredth, time, he said (we were in the carriage alone together) 'To the minute, to the very minute! It's a marvellous thing, the railway; a wonderful age!'

Now I had been long annoyed by the old gentleman's smiling face, platitudes, and piles of newspapers; I had no love for the Age.

'Allow me to tell you,' I said, 'that I consider it a wretched, an ignoble age. Where's the greatness of Life, where's dignity, leisure, stateliness; where's Art and Eloquence? Where are your great scholars, statesmen? Let me ask you, Sir,' I glared at him, 'where's your Gibbon, your Burke or Chatham?'

TRIVIA

Book Two

'Thou, Trivia, Goddess, aid my song,
Thro' spacious streets conduct thy bard along.'

*Trivia: or, the Art of Walking the
Streets of London.* BY MR. GAY.

T R I V I A

L'Oiseau Bleu

What is it, I have more than once asked myself, what is it that I'm looking for in my walks about London? Sometimes it seems to me as if I were following a Bird, a bright Bird which sings divinely as it floats about from one place to another.

When I find myself, however, among persons of middle age and steady principles, see them moving regularly to their offices—what keeps them going? I wonder. And then I feel ashamed of myself and my Bird.

There is though a Philosophic Doctrine—I studied it at College, and I know that many serious people believe it—which maintains that all men, in spite of appearances and pretensions, all live alike for Pleasure. This theory certainly brings portly, respected persons very near to me. Indeed, sometimes with a sense of low complicity I have watched a Bishop. Was that Divine, too, on the hunt for Pleasure, solemnly pursuing his Bird?

At the Bank

Entering the Bank in a composed manner, I drew a cheque and handed it to the cashier through the grating. Then I eyed him narrowly. Would not that astute official see that I was posing as a Real Person? No; he calmly opened a little drawer, took out some real sovereigns, counted them carefully, and handed them to me in a brass shovel. I went away feeling I had perpetrated a delightful fraud. I had got some of the gold of the actual world!

Yet now and then, at the sight of my name on a visiting card, or of my face photographed in a group among other faces, or when I see a letter addressed in my hand, or catch the sound of my own voice, I grow shy in the presence of a mysterious Person who is myself, is known by my name, and who apparently does exist. Can it be possible that I am as real as anyone, and that all of us—the cashier and banker at the Bank, the King on his throne—all feel ourselves ghosts and goblins in this authentic world?

Mammon

Moralists and Church Fathers have named it the root of all Evil, the begetter of hate and bloodshed, the sure cause of the soul's damnation. It has been called 'trash,' 'muck,' 'dunghill excrement,' by grave authors. The love of it is denounced in all Sacred Writings; we find it reprehended on Chaldean bricks, and in the earliest papyri. Buddha, Confucius, Christ, set their faces against it; and they have been followed in more modern times by beneficed Clergymen, Sunday School Teachers, and the leaders of the Higher Thought. But have all the condemnations of all the Saints and Sages done anything to tarnish that bright lustre? Men dig ever deeper into the earth's entrails, travel in search of it farther and farther to arctic and unpleasant regions.

In spite of all my moral reading, I must say I do like to have some of this gaudy substance in my pocket. Its presence cheers and comforts me, diffuses a genial warmth through my body. My eyes rejoice in the shine of it; its clinquant sound is musical in my ears. Since I then am in his paid service, and reject none of the doles of his bounty, I too dwell in the House of Mammon. I bow before the Idol, and taste the unhallowed ecstasy.

How many Altars have been thrown down, and how many Theologies and heavenly Dreams have had their bottoms knocked out of them, while He has sat there, a great God, golden and adorned, secure on His unmoved throne?

Appearance and Reality

It is pleasant to saunter out in the morning sun and idle along the summer streets with no purpose.

But is it Right?

I am not really bothered by these Questions—the hoary old puzzles of Ethics and Philosophy, which lurk around the London corners to waylay me. I have got used to them; and the most formidable of all, the biggest bug of Metaphysics, the Problem which nonplusses the wisest heads on this Planet, has become quite a familiar companion of mine. What is Reality? I ask myself almost daily: how does the External World exist, materialized in mid-air, apart from my perceptions? This show of streets and skies, of policemen and perambulators and hard pavements, is it nothing more than a mere hypothesis and figment of the Mind, or does it remain there, permanent and imposing, when I stop looking at it?

Often, as I saunter along Piccadilly or Bond Street, I please myself with the Berkeleian notion that Matter has no existence, that this so solid-seeming World is all idea, all appearance—that I am carried soft through space inside an immense Thought-bubble, a floating, diaphanous, opal-tinted Dream.

In the Street

These oglings and eye-encounters in the street, little touches of love-liking; faces that ask, as they pass, 'Are you my new lover?' Shall I one day—in Park Lane or Oxford Street perhaps—see the unknown Face I dread and look for?

I See the World

'But you go nowhere, see nothing of the world,' my cousins said.

Now though I do go sometimes to the parties to which I am now and then invited, I find, as a matter of fact, that I get really much more pleasure by looking in at windows, and have a way of my own of seeing the World. And of summer evenings, when cars hurry through the late twilight, and the great houses take on airs of inscrutable expectation, I go owling out through the dusk; and wandering toward the West, lose my way in unknown streets—an unknown City of revels. And when a door opens and a be-diamonded Lady moves to her motor over carpets unrolled by powdered footmen, I can easily think her some great Courtezan, or some half-believed-in Duchess, hurrying to card-tables and candelabra and licentious scenes of joy. I like to see that there are still splendid people on this flat earth; and at dances, standing in the street with the crowd, and stirred by the music, the lights, the rushing sound of voices, I think the Ladies as beautiful as Stars who move up lanes of light into those Palaces; the young men look like Lords in novels; and if (it has once or twice happened) people I know go by me, they strike me as changed and rapt beyond my sphere. And when on hot nights windows are left open, and I can look in at Dinner Parties, as I peer through lace curtains and window-flowers at the silver, the women's shoulders, the shimmer of their jewels, and the divine attitudes of their heads as they lean and listen, I imagine extraordinary intrigues and unheard-of wines and passions.

Social Success

The servant gave me my coat and hat, and in a glow of self-satisfaction I walked out into the night. 'A delightful evening,' I reflected, 'the nicest kind of people. What I said about finance and philosophy impressed them; and how they laughed when I imitated a pig squealing.'

But soon after, 'God, it's awful,' I muttered, 'I wish I was dead.'

Apotheosis

But oh, those heavenly moments when I feel this three-dimensional universe too narrow to contain my Attributes; when a sense of the divine Ipseity invades me; when I know that my voice is the voice of Truth, and my umbrella God's umbrella!

The Goat

In the midst of my anecdote a sudden misgiving chilled me;—had I told them about this Goat before? And then as I talked there gaped upon me—abyss opening beneath abyss—a darker speculation: when goats are mentioned, do I automatically and always tell this story about the Goat at Portsmouth?

Longevity

'But when you are as old as I am!' I said to the young lady in pink satin.

'But I don't know how old you are,' the young lady in pink answered almost archly. We were getting on quite nicely.

'Oh, I'm endlessly old; my memory goes back almost for ever. I come out of the Middle Ages. I am the primitive savage we are all descended from; I believe in Devil-worship and the power of the Stars; I dance under the new Moon, naked and tattooed and holy. I am a Cave-dweller, a contemporary of Mastodons and Mammoths; I am pleistocene and eolithic, and full of the lusts and terrors of the great pre-glacial forests. But that's nothing; I am millions of years older; I am an arboreal Ape, an aged Baboon, with all its instincts; I am a pre-simian quadruped, I have great claws, eyes that see in the dark, and a long prehensile tail.'

'Good gracious!' said the terrified young lady in pink satin. Then she turned away and talked in a hushed voice with her other neighbour.

In the Bus

As I sat inside that crowded bus, so sad, so incredible and sordid seemed the fat face of the woman opposite me, that I interposed the thought of Kilimanjaro, that highest peak of Africa, between us; the grassy slopes and green Arcadian realms of Negro kings from which its dark cone rises; the immense, dim, elephant-haunted forests which clothe its flanks, and above, the white crown of snow, freezing in eternal isolation over the palm trees and deserts of the African Equator.

Daydream

In the cold and malicious society in which I live, I must never mention the Soul, nor speak of my aspirations. If I ever once let these people get a glimpse of the higher side of my nature, they would tear me in pieces.

I wish I had soulful friends—refined Maiden Ladies with ideals and long noses, who live at Hampstead or Putney, and play Chopin with passion. On sad autumn afternoons I would go and have tea with them, and talk of the spiritual meaning of Beethoven's posthumous quartettes, or discuss in the twilight the pathos of life and the Larger Hope.

Providence

But God sees me; He knows my beautiful nature, and how pure I keep amid all sorts of quite horrible temptations. And that is why, as I feel in my bones, there is a special Providence watching over me; an Angel sent expressly from heaven to guide my footsteps from harm. For I never trip up or fall downstairs like other people; I am not run over by cabs and busses at street-crossings; in the worst wind my hat never blows off.

And if ever any of the great cosmic processes or powers threaten me, I believe that God sees it. 'Stop it!' He shouts from His ineffable Throne, 'Don't you touch my Chosen One, my Pet Lamb, my Beloved. Leave him alone, I tell you!'

The Saying of a Persian Poet

All this hurry to dress and go out, these journeys in taxicabs, or in trains with my packed bag from big railway stations—what keeps us going, I sometimes ask my Soul; and I remember how, in his 'Masnavi I Ma'navi' or 'Spiritual Couplets,' Jalalu 'D-Din Muhammad Rumi tells

46

us that the swarm of gaudy Thoughts we pursue and follow are short-lived like summer insects, and must all be killed before long by the winter of age.

Monotony

Oh, to be becalmed on a sea of glass all day; to listen all day to rain on the roof, or the wind in pine trees; to sit all day by a waterfall reading the 'Faërie Queene,' or exquisite, artificial, monotonous Persian poems about an oasis garden where it is always spring—where roses bloom, and lovers sigh, and nightingales lament without ceasing, and groups of white-robed figures sit by the running water and discuss all day, and day after day, the Meaning of Life.

The Spring in London

London seemed last winter like an underground city; as if its low sky were the roof of a cave, and its murky day a light such as one reads of in countries beneath the earth.

And yet the natural sunlight sometimes shone there; unenduring clouds whitened the blue sky; the interminable multitudes of roofs were washed with silver by the Moon, or mantled in snow. And the coming of Spring to London was not unlike the descent of the maiden-goddess into Death's Kingdoms, when pink almond blossoms blew about her in the gloom, and those shadowy people were stirred with faint longings for meadows and the shepherd's life. Nor is there anything more virginal and fresh in wood or orchard, than the shimmer of young foliage, which, in May, dims with delicate green all the smoke-blackened London trees.

Fashion Plates

I like loitering at the bookstalls, looking in at the windows of print-shops, and romancing over the pictures I see of shepherdesses and old-fashioned Beauties. Tall and slim and crowned with plumes in one period, in another these Ladies become as wide-winged as butterflies, or float, large, balloon-like visions, along summer streets. And yet in all shapes they have always (I tell myself) created thrilling effects of beauty, and wakened in the breasts of modish young men ever the same charming Emotion.

But then I have questioned this. Is the emotion always precisely the same? Can one truly say that the human heart remains quite unchanged beneath all the ever-changing fashions of frills and ruffles? In this elegant and cruel Sentiment, I rather fancy that colour and shape do make a difference. I have a notion that about 1840 was the Zenith, the Meridian Hour, the Golden Age of the Passion. Those tight-waisted, whiskered Beaux, those crino-lined Beauties, must have adored one another, I believe, with a leisure, a refinement, and dismay not quite attainable at other dates.

Mental Vice

There are certain hackneyed Thoughts that will force themselves on me; I find my mind, especially in hot weather, buzzed about by moral Platitudes. 'That shows—' I say to myself, or, 'How true it is—' or, 'I really ought to have known!' The sight of a large clock sets me off into musings on the flight of Time; a steamer on the Thames or lines of telegraph inevitably suggest the benefits of Civilization, man's triumph over Nature, the heroism of Inventors, the courage amid ridicule and poverty, of Stephenson and Watt. Like faint, rather unpleasant smells, these thoughts lurk about railway stations. I can hardly post a letter without marvelling at the excellence and accuracy of the Postal System.

Then the pride in the British Constitution and British Freedom, which comes over me when I see, even in the distance, the Towers of Westminster Palace—it is not much comfort that this should be chastened, as I walk down the Embankment, by the sight of Cleopatra's Needle, and the Thought that it will no doubt witness the Fall of the British, as it has that of other Empires, remaining to point its Moral, as old as Egypt, to Antipodeans musing on the dilapidated bridges.

I am sometimes afraid of finding that there is a moral for everything; that the whole great frame of the Universe has a key, like a box; has been contrived and set going by a well-meaning but humdrum Eighteenth-century Creator. It would be a kind of Hell, surely, a world in which everything could be at once explained, shown to be obvious and useful. I am sated with Lesson and Allegory; weary of monitory ants, industrious bees, and preaching animals. The benefits of Civilization cloy me. I have seen enough shining of the didactic Sun.

So gazing up on hot summer nights at the London stars, I cool my thoughts with a vision of the giddy, infinite, meaningless waste of Creation, the blazing Suns, the Planets and frozen Moons, all crashing blindly for ever across the void of space.

Loneliness

Is there, then, no friend? No one who hates Ibsen and problem plays, and the Supernatural, and Switzerland and Adultery as much as I do? Must I live all my life as mute as a mackerel, companionless and uninvited, and never tell anyone what I think of my famous contemporaries? Must I plough always a solitary furrow, and tread the winepress alone?

The Organ of Life

Almost always in London—in the congregated uproar of streets, or in the noise that drifts through walls and windows—you can hear the hackneyed melancholy of street-music; a music which sounds like the actual voice of the human Heart, singing the lost joys, the regrets, the loveless lives of the people who blacken the pavements, or jolt along on the busses.

'Speak to me kindly,' the hand-organ implores; 'I'm all alone!' it screams amid the throng; 'thy Vows are all broken,' it laments in dingy courtyards, 'And light is thy Fame.' And of hot summer afternoons, the Cry for Courage to Remember, or Calmness to Forget, floats in with the smell of paint and asphalt through open office windows.

Humiliation

'My own view is,' I began, but no one listened. At the next pause, 'I always say,' I remarked, but again the loud talk went on. Someone told a story. When the laughter had ended, 'I often think—'; but looking around the table I could catch no friendly, no quickening eye. It was humiliating, but more humiliating the thought that Sophocles and Goethe would have always commanded attention, while the lack of it would not have troubled Spinoza, nor Abraham Lincoln.

Green Ivory

What a bore it is, waking up in the morning always the same person. I wish I were unflinching and emphatic, and had big, bushy eyebrows and a Message for the Age. I wish I were a deep Thinker, or a great Ventriloquist.

I should like to be refined-looking and melancholy, the victim of a hopeless passion; to love in the old, stilted way, with impossible Adoration and Despair under the pale-faced Moon.

I wish I could get up; I wish I were the world's greatest living Violinist. I wish I had lots of silver, and first Editions, and green ivory.

The Correct

I am sometimes visited by a suspicion that everything isn't quite all right with the Righteous; that the Moral Law speaks in oddly equivocal tones to those who listen most scrupulously for its dictates. I feel sure I have detected a look of misgiving in the eyes of its more earnest upholders.

But there is no such shadow or cloud on the faces in Club windows, or in the eyes of drivers of four-in-hands, or of fashionable young men walking down Piccadilly. For these Guardsmen live by a Rule which has not been drawn down from questionable skies, and needs no sanction. What they do is Correct, and that is all. Correctly dressed from head to foot, they pass, with correct thought and gestures, exchanging correct remarks, correctly across the Earth's roundness.

'Where Do I Come In?'

When I read in the *Times* about India and all its problems and populations; when I look at the letters in large type of important personages, and find myself face to face with the Questions, Movements, and great Activities of the Age, 'Where do I come in?' I ask uneasily.

Then in the great *Times*-reflected world I find the corner where I play my humble but necessary part. For I am one of the unpraised, unrewarded millions without whom Statistics would be a bankrupt science. It is we who are born, who marry, who die, in constant ratios; who regularly lose so many umbrellas, post just so many unaddressed letters every year. And there are enthusiasts among us, Heroes who, without the least thought of their own convenience, allow omnibuses to run over them, or throw themselves, great-heartedly, month by month, in fixed numbers, from the London bridges.

Microbes

But how is one to keep free from those mental microbes that worm-eat people's brains—those Theories and Diets and Enthusiasms and infectious Doctrines that we catch from what seem the most innocuous contacts? People go about laden with germs; they breathe creeds and convictions on you as soon as they open their mouths. Books and newspapers are simply creeping with them—the monthly Reviews seem to have room for little else. Wherewithal then shall a young man cleanse his way; how shall he keep his mind immune to Theosophical speculations, and novel schemes of Salvation? Can he ever be sure that he won't be suddenly struck down by the fever of Funeral or of Spelling Reform, or take to his bed with a new Sex Theory?

But is this struggle for a healthy mind in a maggoty

world really after all worth it? Are there not soporific dreams and sweet deliriums more soothing than Reason? If Transmigration can make clear the dark Problem of Evil; if Mrs. Mary Baker Eddy can free us from Death; if the belief that Bacon wrote Shakespeare gives a peace which the world cannot give, why pedantically reject such solace? Why not be led with the others by still waters, be made to lie down in green pastures?

The Quest

'We walk alone in the world,' the Moralist writes in his essay on Ideal Friendship, somewhat sadly. 'Friends such as we desire are dreams and fables.' Yet we never quite give up the hope of finding them. But what awful things happen to us, what snubs, what set-downs we experience, what shames and disillusions. We can never really tell what these new unknown persons may do to us. Sometimes they seem nice, and then begin to talk like gramophones. Sometimes they grab at us with moist hands, or breathe hotly on our necks, or make awful confidences, or drench us from sentimental slop-pails. And too often, among the thoughts in the loveliest heads, we come on nests of woolly caterpillars.

And yet we brush our hats, pull on our gloves, and go out and ring door-bells.

The Kaleidoscope

I find in my mind, on its background of ideas and musings, a curious moving screen of little landscapes, shining and fading for no reason. Sometimes they are views in no way remarkable—the corner of a road, a heap of stones, an old gate. But there are many charming pictures too: as I read, between my eyes and book, the Moon washes the harvest-fields with her chill of silver; I see autumnal avenues, with the leaves falling, or swept in heaps; and storms blow among my thoughts, with the rain beating for ever on the fields. Then Winter's upward glare of snow brightens; or the pink and delicate green of Spring in the windy sunshine; or cornfields and green waters, and youths bathing in Summer's golden heat.

And as I walk about, places haunt me; a cathedral rises above a dark blue foreign town, the colour of ivory in the sunset light; now I find myself in a French garden, full of lilacs and bees, and shut-in sunshine, with the Mediterranean lounging outside its walls; now in a little college library, with busts, and the green reflected light of Oxford lawns;—and again I hear the bells, reminding me of the Oxford hours.

The Abbey at Night

And as at night I went past the Abbey, saw its walls towering high and solemn among the Autumn stars, I pictured to myself the white population in the vast darkness of its interior—all that hushed people of Heroes—; not dead, I would think them, but animated with a still kind of life, and at last, after all their intolerable toils, the sounding tumult of battle, and perilous sea-paths, resting there, tranquil and satisfied and glorious, amid the epitaphs and allegorical figures of their tombs;—those high-piled, trophied, shapeless Abbey tombs, that long ago they toiled for, and laid down their gallant lives to win.

Oxford Street

One late winter afternoon in Oxford Street, amid the noise of vehicles and voices that filled that dusky thoroughfare, as I was borne onward with the crowd past the great electric-lighted shops, a holy Indifference filled my thoughts. Illusion had faded from me; I was not touched by any desire for the goods displayed in those golden windows, nor had I the smallest share in the appetites and fears of all those moving faces. And as I listened with Asiatic detachment to the London traffic, its sound changed into something ancient and dissonant and sad—into the turbid flow of that stream of Craving which sweeps men onward through the meaningless cycles of Existence, blind and enslaved for ever. But I had reached the farther shore, the Harbour of Deliverance, the Holy City; the Great Peace beyond all this turmoil and fret compassed me around. *Om Mani padme hum*—I murmured the sacred syllables, smiling with the pitying smile of the Enlightened One on his heavenly lotus.

56

Then, in a shop-window, I saw a neatly fitted suit-case. I liked that suit-case; I wanted it. Immediately I was enveloped by the mists of Illusion, chained once more to the Wheel of Existence, whirled onward along Oxford Street in that turbid stream of wrong-belief, and lust, and sorrow, and anger.

Beauty

Among all the ugly mugs of the world we see now and then a face made after the divine pattern. Then, a wonderful thing happens, the Blue Bird sings, the golden Splendour shines, and for a queer moment everything seems meaningless save our impulse to follow those fair forms, to follow them to the clear Paradises they promise.

Plato assures us that these moments are not (as we are apt to think them) mere blurs and delusions of the senses, but divine revelations; that in a lovely face we see imaged, as in a mirror, the Absolute Beauty—; it is Reality, flashing on us in the cave where we dwell amid shadows and darkness. Therefore we should follow these fair forms, says he, and their shining footsteps will lead us upward to the highest heaven of Wisdom. The Poets, too, keep chanting this doctrine of Beauty in grave notes to their golden strings. The music floats up through the skies so sweet, so strange, that the very Angels seem to lean from their stars to listen.

But, O Plato, O Shelley, O Angels of Heaven, what scrapes, what scrapes you do get us into!

The Power of Words

I thanked the club porter who helped me into my coat, and stepped out gayly into the vasty Night. And as I walked along my eyes were dazzling with the glare behind me; I heard the sound of my speech, the applause and laughter.

And when I looked up at the Stars, the great Stars that bore me company, streaming over the dark houses as I moved, I felt that I was the Lord of Life; the mystery and disquieting meaninglessness of existence—the existence of other peole, and of my own—were solved for me now. As for the Earth, hurrying beneath my feet, how bright was its journey; how shining the goal toward which it went swinging—you might really say leaping—through the sky.

'I must tell the Human Race of this!' I heard my voice; saw my prophetic gestures, as I expounded the ultimate meaning of existence to the white, rapt faces of Humanity. Only to find the words—that troubled me; were there then no words to describe this Vision—divine—intoxicating?

And then the Word struck me; the Word people would use. I stopped in the street; my Soul was silenced like a bell that snarls at a jarring touch. I stood there awhile and meditated on language, its perfidious meanness, the inadequacy, the ignominy of our vocabulary, and how Moralists have spoiled our words by distilling into them, as into little vials of poison, all their hatred of human joy.

Away with that police-force of brutal words which bursts

ın on our best moments and arrests our finest feelings! This music within me, large, like the song of the stars—like a Glory of Angels singing,—'No one has any right to say I am drunk!' I shouted.

Self-analysis

'Yes, aren't they odd, the thoughts that float through one's mind for no reason? But why not be frank?—I suppose the best of us are shocked at times by the things we find ourselves thinking. Don't you agree,' I went on, not noticing (until it was too late) that all other conversation had ceased, and the whole dinner-party was listening, 'don't you agree that the oddest of all are the bawdy thoughts that come into one's head—the unspeakable words, I mean, and Obscenities?'

When I remember this occasion, I immediately think of Space, and the unimportance in its unmeasured vastness of our toy solar system; I lose myself in speculations on Eternity, reflecting how, at the best, human life on this minute and perishable planet is but a mock episode, as brief as a dream.

The Voice of the World

'And what are you doing now?' The question of these school contemporaries of mine, and their greeting the other day in Piccadilly (I remember how shabby I felt as I stood talking to them)—for a day or two that question haunted me. And behind their well-bred voices I seemed to hear the voice of Schoolmasters and Tutors, of the Professional Classes, and indeed of all the World.

What, as a plain matter of fact, was I doing? how did I spend my days? The life-days which I knew were numbered, and which were described in sermons and on tombstones as so irrevocable, so melancholy-brief.

I decided to change my life. I too would be somebody in my time and age; the world should hear of me; my contemporaries should treat me as an important person. I began thinking of my endeavours, my studies by the midnight lamp, my risings at dawn for stolen hours of self-improvement.

But alas, the Day, the little Day, was enough just then. It somehow seemed enough, just to be alive in the Spring, with the young green of the trees, the smell of smoke in the sunshine; I loved the old shops and books, the uproar darkening and brightening in the shabby daylight. Just a run of good-looking faces—I was always looking for faces —would keep me amused. All London was but a dim-lit stage on which I played the part I liked. I would wake up in the morning like Byron to find myself famous; be drawn like Chatham to St. Paul's, amid the cheers of the Nation, and exclaim with Cromwell, 'Take away that bauble!' as I stalked past the Houses of Parliament.

And Anyhow

And anyhow, soon, so soon (in only two thousand million years or thereabouts, the Encyclopaedia said) this Earth would grow cold, all human activities end, and the last wretched mortals close their eyes on the rays of the dying Sun.

Drawbacks

I should be all right. . . .

If it weren't for these sudden visitations of Happiness, these downpourings of Heaven's blue, little invasions of Paradise, or waftings to the Happy Islands, or whatever you may call these disconcerting Moments, I should be like everybody else; as blameless a ratepayer as any in our Row.

Talk

Once in a while, when doors are closed and curtains drawn on a group of free spirits, the miracle happens, and Good Talk begins. 'Tis a sudden illumination—the glow, it may be, of sanctified tapers, or more likely, the blaze around a cauldron of wicked gossip.

Is there an ecstasy or any intoxication like it? Oh, to talk, to talk people into monsters, and carve them as dishes for the Gods; to talk one's self out of one's clothes, to talk Jehovah from His high Heaven, to say everything, and turn everything in the world into a bright tissue of phrases!

These Pentecosts and outpourings of the spirit can only

occur very rarely, or the Universe itself would be soon talked out of existence.

The Church of England

I have my Anglican moments; and as I sat there that Sunday afternoon, in the eighteenth-century interior of the London Church, and listened to the unexpressive voices chanting the correct service, I felt a comfortable assurance that we were in no danger of being betrayed into any unseemly manifestations of religious fervour. We had not gathered together at that performance to abase ourselves obsequiously, with furious hosannas before any dark Creator of an untamed Universe, no Deity of freaks and miracles and sinister hocus-pocus; but to pay our duty to a highly respected Anglican First Cause—distinguished, undemonstrative, gentlemanly—whom, without loss of self-respect, we could decorously praise.

Misgiving

We were talking of people, and a name familiar to us all was mentioned. We paused and looked at each other; then soon, by means of anecdotes and clever touches, that Personality was reconstructed, and seemed to appear before us, large, pink, and life-like, and give a comic sketch of itself with characteristic poses.

What fun it was! 'But of course,' I said to myself, 'this sort of thing never happens to me.' For the notion was quite unthinkable, the notion, I mean, of my own dear Imago, called up like this without my knowledge, to turn my discreet way of life into a cake-walk.

⚔ Sanctuaries

She said, 'How small the world is, after all!'

I thought of China, of a holy mountain in the West of China, full of legends and sacred groves and demon-haunted caves. It is always enveloped in mountain mists; through that white thick air the faint sound of bells reach me, the muffled footsteps of innumerable pilgrims, and the reiterated mantra, *Nam-Mo, O-mi-to-Fo,* which they murmur as they climb its slopes. High up among its temples and monasteries march processions of monks, with chants and services, and many prostrations, and lighted candles that glimmer through the fog. There in their solemn shrines stand the statues of the Arahats, and there, seated on his white elephant, looms immense and dim, the image of Amitabha, the Lord of the Western Heavens.

She said, 'Life is so complicated!'

Climbing inaccessible cliffs of rock and ice, I shut myself within a Tibetan monastery beyond the Himalayan ramparts. I join with choirs of monks, intoning their deep sonorous dirges and unintelligible prayers; I beat drums, I clash cymbals, and blow at dawn from the Lamasery roofs conches, and loud discordant trumpets. And wandering through those vast and shadowy halls, as I tend the butter-lamps of the golden Buddhas, and watch the storms that sweep across the barren mountains, I taste an imaginary bliss, and then pass on to other scenes and incarnations along the endless road that leads me to Nirvana.

'But I do wish you would tell me what you really think?'

I flee to Africa, into the depths of the dark Ashanti forest. There, in its gloomiest recesses, where the soil is stained with the blood of the Negroes He has eaten, dwells that monstrous Deity of human shape and red colour, the great Fetish God, Sasabonsum. I like Sasabonsum: other Gods are sometimes moved to pity, to forgiveness, but to Him such weakness is unknown. He is utterly and absolutely implacable; no prayers, no human sacrifices can ever for one moment appease His cold, malignant rage.

Symptoms

'But there are certain people I simply can't put up with. A dreariness and sense of death come over me when I meet them—I really find it difficult to breathe when they are in the room, as if they had pumped all the air out of it. Wouldn't it be dreadful to produce that effect on people! But they never seem to be aware of it. I remember once meeting a famous Bore; I really must tell you about it, it shows the unbelievable obtuseness of such people.'

I told this and another story or two with great gusto, and talked on of my experiences and sensations, till suddenly I noticed, in the appearance of my charming neighbour, something—a slightly glazed look in her eyes, a just perceptible irregularity in her breathing—which turned that occasion for me suddenly into a Nightmare.

Shadowed

I sometimes feel a little uneasy about that imagined self of mine—the Me of my daydreams—who leads a melodramatic life of his own, out of all relation with my real existence. So one day I shadowed him down the street. He loitered along for a while, and then stood at a shop-window and dressed himself out in a gaudy tie and yellow waistcoat. Then he bought a great sponge and two stuffed birds and took them to lodgings, where he led a shady existence. Next he moved to a big house in Mayfair, and gave grand dinner-parties, with splendid service and costly wines. His amorous encounters among the High-up Ones of this Earth I pass over. He soon sold his house and horses, gave up his motors, dismissed his retinue of servants, and went— saving two young ladies from being run over on the way— to live a life of heroic self-sacrifice among the poor.

I was beginning to feel encouraged about this person, when in passing a fishmonger's, he pointed at a great salmon with his stick on the slab, and said, 'I caught that fish.'

The Incredible

'Yes, but they were afraid of you.'
'Afraid of *me*?'
'Yes, so one of them told me afterwards.'

I was fairly jiggered. If my personality can inspire fear or respect, the world must be a simpler place than I had thought it. Afraid of a twittering shadow, a make-believe like me? Are children more phantasmagorically terrified by a candle in a hollow turnip? Was Bedlam at full moon ever scared by anything half so silly?

Terror

A pause suddenly fell on our conversation—one of those uncomfortable lapses when we sit with fixed smiles, searching our minds for some remark with which to fill up the unseasonable silence. It was only a moment—'But suppose,' I said to myself with horrible curiosity, 'suppose none of use had found a word to say?'

It is the dread of Something happening, Something monstrously awful, that makes us do anything to keep the flicker of talk from dying out. So travellers at night in an unknown forest keep their fire ablaze, in fear of Wild Beasts lurking in the darkness ready to leap upon them.

Pathos

When winter twilight falls in my street with the rain, a sense of the horrible sadness of life descends upon me. I think of drunken old women who drown themselves because nobody loves them; I think of Napoleon at St. Helena, and of Byron, growing irritable and fat in the enervating climate of Italy.

Inconstancy

The rose that one wears and throws away, the friend one forgets, the music that passes;—out of the well-known transitoriness of mortal things I have made myself a maxim or precept to the effect that it is foolish to look for one face, or to listen long for one voice, in a world that is, after all, as I know, full of enchanting voices.

But all the same, I can never quite forget the enthusiasm with which, as a boy, I read the praises of Constancy, of True Love and the unchanged Northern Star.

The Poplar

There is a great tree in Sussex, whose cloud of blue foliage floats high in the summer air. The thrush sings in that cool umbrage, and blackbirds, who fill the late, decorative sunshine with a shimmer of golden sound. There the nightingale finds her green cloister; and on those branches sometimes, like a great fruit, hangs the lemon-coloured Moon. In the glare of August, when all the world is faint with heat, there is always a breeze in those cool recesses; always a noiseless noise, like the noise of water, among their lightly-hung leaves.

But the owner of this Tree lives in London, and dines out.

On the Doorstep

I rang the bell as of old; as of old I gazed at the great shining Door and waited. But, alas! that flutter and beat of the wild heart, that delicious Doorstep Terror—it was gone; and with it dear, fantastic, panic-stricken Youth had rung the bell, flitted around the corner and vanished for ever.

The Moon

I went in and shook hands with my hostess, but no one screamed or left the room; the quiet murmur of talk went on. I suppose I seemed like the others; observed from outside no doubt I looked like them.

But inside, seen from within . . . ? Or was it conceivable that all these quietly-talking people had got the Moon, too, in their heads?

Consolation

The other day, depressed on the Undergound, I tried to cheer myself by thinking over the joys of our human lot. But there wasn't one of them for which I seemed to care a button—not Wine, nor Fame, nor Friendship, nor Eating, nor Making Love, nor the Consciousness of Virtue. Was it worth while then going way up in a lift into a world that had nothing less trite to offer?

Then I thought of reading—the nice and subtle happiness of reading. This was enough, this joy not dulled by

Age, this polite and unpunishable vice, this selfish, serene, life-long intoxication.

The Lord Mayor

An arctic wind was blowing; it cut through me as I stood there. The boot-black was finishing his work and complaints.

'But I should be 'appy, sir, if only I could make four bob a day,' he said.

I looked down at him; it seemed absurd, the belief of this crippled, half-frozen creature. Happiness! the fabled treasure of some far-away heaven; not to be bought with gold, not of this earth!

I said something to this effect. But four shillings a day was enough for the boot-black.

'Why, sir,' he said, 'I should be as 'appy as the Lord Mayor!'

The Burden

I know too much; I have stuffed too many of the facts of History and Science into my intellectuals. My eyes have grown dim over books; believing in geological periods, cave-dwellers, Chinese Dynasties, and the fixed Stars has prematurely aged me.

Why am I to blame for all that is wrong in the world? I didn't invent Sin and Hate and Slaughter. Who made it my duty anyhow to administer the Universe, and keep the planets to their courses? My Atlantean shoulders are bent beneath the load of the Firmament; I grow weary of bearing the weight of the whole World.

Under an Umbrella

From under the roof of my umbrella I saw the washed pavement lapsing beneath my feet, the news-posters lying smeared with dirt at the crossings, the tracks of the busses in the liquid mud. On I went through this world of wetness. And through what long perspectives of the years shall I still hurry down wet streets—middle-aged, and then, perhaps, very old? And on what errands?

Asking myself this question I fade from your vision, Reader, into the distance, sloping my umbrella against the wind.

MORE TRIVIA

The Epithet

'Night-wandering, lucid, honey-pale—or blanc, as Milton called her—'

The morning paper lay there unopened; I knew I ought to look at the news, for the crash was awful, but I was too busy just then trying to find an adjective for the Moon —the magical, moony epithet, which could I only find or invent, what then would matter the quakes and sublunary conflicts of this negligible earth?

Reassurance

I look at my overcoat and my hat hanging in the hall with reassurance; for although I go out of doors with one individuality today, when yesterday I had quite another, yet my clothes keep my various selves buttoned up together, and enable all these otherwise irreconcilable aggregates of psychological phenomena to pass themselves off as one person.

The Great Adventure

I paused, before opening the front-door, for a moment of deep consideration.

Dim-lit, shadowy, full of menace and unimaginable

chances, stretched all around my door the many-peopled streets. I could hear, ominous and muffled, the tides of traffic, sounding multitudinously along their ways. Was I equipped for the navigation of those waters, armed and ready to adventure out into that dangerous world again?

Gloves? Money? Cigarettes? Matches? Yes; and I had an umbrella for its tempests, and a latchkey for my safe return.

The Beatific Vision

Shoving and pushing, and pushed and shoved, a dishonoured bag of bones about London, or carted like a herring in a box through tunnels in the clay beneath it, as I bump my head in an omnibus, or hang, half-suffocated, from a greasy strap in the Underground, I dream, like other Idealists and Saints and Social Thinkers, of a better world than this, a world that might be, a City of Heaven brought down at last to earth.

One footman flings open the portals of my palace in that New Jerusalem for me; another unrolls a red path of velvet to the enormous motor which floats me through the city traffic—I leaning back like Edward VII, or like God, on leather cushions, smoking a big cigar.

Faces

Almost always the streets are full of dingy people; sometimes for weeks on end the poor face-hunter returns unblest from his expeditions, with no provision with which to replenish his daydream-larder.

Then one day the plenty is all too great; there are Princesses at the street-crossings, Queens in the taxi-cabs, Beings fair as the dayspring on the tops of busses; and the Gods themselves promenade up and down Piccadilly.

The Observer

Talks of ants! It's the precise habits, the incredible proceedings of human insects I like to note and study.

Walking today, a stranger dropped upon this planet, towards Victoria, a funny thing happened to me. I chanced to see a female of this species, a certain Mrs. Jones of my acquaintance, approaching from the opposite direction, and immediately I found myself performing the oddest set of movements. I straightened my back and simpered, I lifted my hat in the air; and then, seizing the cinquedigitated paw of this female, I moved it up and down several times, giving utterance to a set formula of articulated sounds.

These anthropological gestures and vocalizations, and my automatic performance of them, reminded me that it was from inside one of them I was observing those Bipeds.

Chaos

Punctual, commonplace, keeping all appointments, as I go my round in the obvious world, a bit of Chaos and old Night lingers on inside me; a dark bewilderment of mind, a nebulous sea of meditation; a looming of speculative universes out of nothing, and their collapse, as in a dream.

The Ghost

When people talk of Ghosts I don't mention the Apparition by which I am haunted, the Phantom that shadows me about the streets, the image or spectre, so familiar, so like myself, which lurks in the plate-glass of shop-windows, or leaps out of mirrors to waylay me.

The Suburbs

What are the beliefs about God in Grosvenor Gardens, the surmises of South Kensington concerning our fate beyond the Grave? On what ground does life seem worth living in Pimlico; and how far in the Cromwell Road do they follow, or think they follow, the precepts of the Sermon on the Mount?

If I can but dimly discern the ideals of these familiar regions, how much more am I in the dark about the inner life of the great outer suburbs. In what works of local introspection can I study the daydreams of Hoxton, the curiosities and discouragements of Camberwell or Ealing?

More than once I have paused before a suburban villa, telling myself that I had after all but to ring the bell, and go in and ask them. But alas, they wouldn't tell me; they couldn't tell me, even if they would.

The Latchkey

I was startled, I was scared by the sight of the New Moon at the end of the street. In Blake-like wonder I stood and gazed at it on my doorstep. For what was I doing there? I, a wanderer, a pilgrim, a nomad of the desert, with no home save where the evening found me;—what was my business on that doorstep? At what commonplace had the Moon caught me with a latchkey in my hand?

⚹ Good Practice

We met in an omnibus last evening. 'And where are you going now?' she asked, as she looked at me with amusement.

'I am going, if the awful truth must be told, to dine in Grosvenor Square.'

'Lord!' she colloquially replied, 'and what do you do that for?'

'I do it because I am invited. And besides,' I went on, 'let me remind you of what the Persian Mystics say of the Saints—that the Saints are sometimes rich, that God sometimes endows Those Holy Ones with an outward show of wealth to hide them from the profane.'

'Oh, does He?;—Hides them in Grosvenor Square?'

'Very well then, I shall tell you the real truth; I shall tell you my real reason for going to dine there. Do you remember what Diogenes replied when they wanted to know why he had begged for money from a statue?'

'No; what did he say?'

'He said;—but I must explain another time. I have to get off here. Good-night.'

I paused, however, at the door of the bus. 'He said,' I called back, ' "I am practising Disappointment." '

Evasion

'And what do you think of the International Situation?' asked that foreign Countess, with her foreign, fascinating smile.

Was she a Spy? I felt I must be careful.

'What do I think?' I evasively echoed; and then, carried away by the profound and melancholy interest of this question, 'Think?' I queried, 'do I ever really think? Is there anything inside me but cotton-wool? How can I, with a mind full of grey monkeys with blue faces, call myself a Thinker? What am I anyhow?' I pursued the sad inquiry: 'A noodle, a pigwidgeon, a ninny-hammer—a bubble on the wave, Madame, a leaf in the wind!'

Dining Out

When I think of Etiquette and Funerals; when I consider the euphemisms and conventions and various costumes with which we invest the acts of our animal existence; when I bear in mind how elegantly we eat our victuals, and remember all the ablutions and preparations and salutations and exclamations and manipulations I per-

formed when I dined out last evening, I reflect what creatures we are of ceremony; how elaborately polite a simian
Species.

What's Wrong

From their corner of the half-empty drawing-room they
could see in a great mirror the other dinner-guests linger
and depart. But none of them were going on—what was
the good?—to that evening party. They talked of satiety
and disenchantment, of the wintry weather, of illness, of
Age and Death.

'But what really frightens me most in life,' said one of
them, 'what gives me a kind of vertigo or shiver, is—it
sounds absurd, but it's simply the horror of space, *l'épou-
vante sidérale*—the dismay of Infinity, the black abysses in
the Milky Way, the silence of those eternal spaces.'

'But Time,' said another of the group, 'surely Time is a
worse nightmare. Think of it! the Past with never a beginning, the Future going on for ever and ever, and the
little Present in which we live, twinkling for a second, between these abysses'

'What's wrong with me,' mused the third speaker, 'is
that even the Present eludes me. I don't know what it really
is; I can never catch the moment as it passes; I am always
far ahead or far away behind, and always somewhere else.
I am not really here now with you. And why should I go
to the party? I shouldn't be there, either, if I went. My life
is all reminiscence and anticipation—if you can call it life,
if I am not rather a kind of ghost, haunting a past that has

ceased to exist, or a future that is still more shadowy. It's ghastly in a way, this exile and isolation. But why speak of it, after all?'

They rose, and their figures too were reflected in the great mirror, as they passed out of the drawing-room, and dispersed, each on his or her way, into the winter night.

Sir Eustace Carr

When I read the news about Sir Eustace Carr in the morning paper, I was startled, like everyone else who knew, if only by name, this young man, whose wealth and good looks, whose adventurous travels and whose brilliant and happy marriage, had made of him an almost romantic figure.

Every now and then one hears of some strange happening of this kind. But they are acts so anomalous, in such startling contradiction to all our usual ways and accepted notions of life and its value, that most of us are willing enough to accept the familiar explanation of insanity, or any other commonplace cause which may be alleged— financial trouble, or some passionate entanglement, and the fear of scandal and exposure. And then the Suicide is forgotten as soon as possible, and his memory shuffled out of the way as something unpleasant to think of. But I sometimes wonder about these cases, asking myself whether the dead man may not have carried to the grave with him the secret of some strange perplexity, some passion or craving or irresistible impulse, of which perhaps his intimates, and certainly the coroner's jury, could have had no inkling.

I had never met or spoken to Sir Eustace Carr—the worlds we lived in were very different—but I had read of his explorations in the East, and of the curious tombs he had discovered—somewhere, was it not?—in the Nile Valley. Then, too, it happened (and this was the main cause of my interest) that at one time I had seen him more than once, under circumstances that were rather unusual. And now I began to think of this incident. In a way it was nothing, and yet the impression haunted me that it was somehow connected with this final act, for which no explanation, beyond that of sudden mental derangement, had been offered. This explanation did not seem to me wholly adequate, although it had been accepted, I believe, both by his friends and the general public—and with the more apparent reason on account of a strain of eccentricity, amounting in some cases almost to insanity which could be traced, it was said, in his mother's family.

I found it not difficult to revive with a certain vividness the memory of those cold and rainy November weeks that I had happened to spend alone, some years ago, in Venice, and of the churches which I had so frequently haunted. Especially I remembered the great dreary church in the *campo* near my lodgings, into which I would often go on my way to my rooms in the twilight. It was the season when all the Venice churches are draped in black, and services for the dead are held in them at dawn and twilight; and when I entered this Baroque interior, with its twisted columns and volutes and high-piled, hideous tombs, adorned with skeletons and allegorical figures and angels blowing trumpets—all so agitated, and yet all so dead and empty and frigid—I would find the fantastic darkness filled with glimmering candles, and kneeling figures, and the discordant noise of chanting. There I would sit, while outside night fell with the rain on Venice; the palaces and green canals faded into darkness, and the great bells, swinging against the low sky, sent the melancholy sound of their voices far over the lagoons.

It was here, in this church, that I used to see Sir Eustace Carr; would generally find him in the same corner when I entered, and would sometimes watch his face, until the ceremonious extinguishing of the candles, one by one, left us in shadowy night. It was a handsome and thoughtful face, and I remember more than once wondering what had brought him to Venice in that unseasonable month, and why he came so regularly to this monotonous service. It was as if some spell had drawn him; and now, with my curiosity newly wakened, I asked myself what had been that spell? I also must have been affected by it, for I had been there also in his uncommunicating company. Here, I felt, was perhaps the answer to my question, the secret of the enigma that puzzled me; and as I went over my memories of that time, and revived its sombre and almost sinister fascination, I seemed to see an answer looming before my imagination. But it was an answer, an hypothesis or supposition, so fantastic, that my common-sense could hardly accept it. For I now sensed that the spell which had been on us both at that time in Venice had been nothing but the spell and tremendous incantation of the Thought of Death. The dreary city with its decaying palaces and great tomb-encumbered churches had really seemed, in those dark and desolate weeks, to be the home and metropolis of the King of Terrors; and the services at dawn and twilight, with their prayers for the Dead, and funereal candles, had been the chanted ritual of his worship. Now suppose (such was the notion that held my imagination) suppose this spell, which I had felt but for a time and dimly, should become to someone a real obsession, casting its shadow more and more completely over a life otherwise prosperous and happy, might not this be the clue to a history like that of Sir Eustace Carr's—not only his interest in the buried East, his presence at that time in Venice, but also his unexplained and mysterious end?

Musing on this half-believed notion, I thought of the great personages and great nations we read of in ancient history, who have seemed to live with a kind of morbid pleasure, sepulchrally, in the shadow of this great Thought; who have surrounded themselves with mementoes of Death, and hideous symbols of its power, and who, like the Egyptians, have found their main interest, not in the present, but in imaginary explorations of the unknown future; not on the sunlit surface of this earth, but in the vaults and dwelling-places of the Dead beneath it.

Since this preoccupation, this curiosity, this nostalgia, has exercised so enormous a fascination in the past, I found it not impossible to imagine some modern favourite of fortune falling a victim to this malady of the soul; until at last, growing weary of other satisfactions, he might be drawn to open for himself the dark portal and join the inhabitants of that dim region. This, as I say, was the notion that haunted me, the link my imagination forged between Sir Eustace Carr's presence in that dark Venetian church, and his death some years later. But whether this is nothing more than a somewhat sinister fancy, of course I can't say.

At a Solemn Music

I sat there, hating the exuberance of her bust, and her high-coloured wig. And how could I listen to hushed music so close to those loud stockings?

Then our eyes met: in both of us the enchanted chord was touched; we both looked through the same window into Heaven. In that moment of musical, shared delight, my soul and the unembodied soul of that large lady joined hands and sang like the Morning Stars together.

The Communion of Souls

'So of course I bought it! How could I help buying it?' Then, lifting the conversation, as with Lady Hyslop one always lifts it, to a higher level, 'this notion of Free Will,' I went on, 'the notion, for instance, that I was free to buy or not to buy that rare edition, seems, when you think of it —at least to me it seems—a wretched notion really. I like to feel that I must follow the things I desire as—how shall I put it?—as the tide follows the Moon; that my actions are due to necessary causes; that the world inside me isn't a meaningless chaos, but a world of order, like the world outside, governed by beautiful laws, as the Stars are governed.'

'Ah, how I love the Stars!' murmured Lady Hyslop. 'What things they say to me! They are the pledges of lost recognition; the promise of ineffable mitigations.'

'Mitigations?' I gasped, feeling a little giddy. But it didn't matter: always when we meet Lady Hyslop and I have the most sublime conversations.

Waxworks

'But one really never knows the Age one lives in. How interesting it would be,' I said to the lady next me, 'how I wish we could see ourselves as Posterity will see us!'

I have said it before; but on this occasion I was struck—almost thunder-struck—by my own remark. Like a rash exorcist, I was appalled by the spirit I had raised myself. For a queer second I did see us all inevitably in that mirror, but cadaverous, palsied, out-of-date,—a dusty set of old waxworks, simpering inanely in the lumber-room of Time.

'Better to be forgotten at once!' I exclaimed, with an emphasis that seemed somewhat to surprise the lady next me.

Adjectives

But why wasn't I born, alas, in an age of Adjectives; why can one no longer write of silver-shedding Tears and moon-tailed Peacocks, of eloquent Death, of the Negro and star-enamelled Night?

Desperance

'Yes, as you say, life is so full of disappointment, disillusion! More and more I ask myself, as I grow older, what is the good of it all? We dress, we go out to dinner,' I went on, 'but surely we walk in a vain show, as the Bible puts it, and are crushed before the moth. How good this asparagus is! I often say asparagus is the most delicious vegetable of all. And yet, I don't know—when one thinks of fresh green peas. One can get tired of asparagus, as one can of strawberries—but I could eat tender peas for ever. Then peaches, and melons;—and there are certain pears, too, that taste like heaven. One of my favourite daydreams for the long evening of my life is to live alone, a formal, greedy, selfish old gentleman, in a square house, say, in Devonshire, with a square garden, whose walls are covered with apricots and figs and peaches: and there are precious pears, too, of my own planting, on espaliers along the paths. I shall walk out with a gold-headed cane in the smoky sunshine, and just at the ripe moment pick another pear. However, that isn't at all what I was going to say—'

Chairs

In the streets of London there are door-bells I ring (I see myself ringing them); in certain houses there are chairs covered with chintz or cretonne in which I sit and talk about life, explaining often after tea what I think of it.

A Grievance

They are all persons of elegant manners and spotless reputations; they seem to welcome my visits, and they listen to my anecdotes with unflinching attention. I have only one grievance against them; they will keep in their houses books full of stale epithets, which, when I only seem to smell their mawkish proximity, produce in me a feeling of nausea.

There are people, I believe, who are affected in this way by the presence of cats.

Misquotation

Some 'precious phrase by all the Muses trimmed,' he quoted.

I knew that the word was 'filed'—'by all the Muses filed' —but I said nothing.

That I should permit a misquotation like this to pass made me doubt my own identity. Or, it occurred to me, my personality might be changing; I was undergoing, perhaps, like an insect in the silence of its cocoon, some curious metamorphosis? I waited to see what I might be turning into—a Low Church Curate? A Major with a big moustache? or a Licensed Victualler, perhaps?

Victoria Street

We were talking of the state of the world as we walked towards Westminster—as we walked and were sad. The outlook, my companion said, was black beyond description.

Just then a gleam of sun gilded the Abbey Towers above the roofs of Victoria Street before us. 'But why,' I asked, as my eyes drank in this shining picture, 'why do we live for anything but Beauty? What is there that gives a meaning to the world but Beauty;—these splendours,' I said, 'that seem to fall upon us from the empyrean, from climes of bliss beyond the Constellations?'

Justification

Well, what if I did put it on a little at that luncheon party? Don't I owe it to my friends to assert now and then my claims to consideration; ought I always to allow myself to be juggernauted, trampled on and treated as dirt? And how about the Saints and Patriarchs of the Bible? Didn't Joseph tell of the dream in which his wheatsheaf was exalted; Deborah sing without blame how she arose a mother in Israel, and David boast of his triumph over the paw of the lion and the bear's paw? Nay, in His confabulations with His chosen people, does not the Creator of the Universe Himself make the most astounding efforts to impress upon those Hebrews His importance, His power, His glory?

Well. wasn't I made in His image?

The Hour-Glass

At the corner of Oakley Street I stopped for a moment's chat with my neighbour, Mrs. Wheble, who was waiting there for a bus.

'Do tell me,' she asked, 'what you have got in that odd-looking parcel?'

'It's an hour-glass,' I said, taking it out of its paper wrapping. 'I've always wanted an hour-glass to measure time by. What a mystery Time really is, when you think of it! See, the sands are running out now while we're talking. I've got here in my hand the most potent, the most enigmatic, the most fleeting of all essences—Time, the sad cure for all our sorrows;—but I say! There's your bus just starting. You'll miss it if you don't look out!'

Action

I am no mere thinker, no mere creature of dreams and imagination. I pay bills, post letters; I buy new bootlaces and put them in my boots. And when I set out to get my hair cut, it is with the iron face of those men of empire

89

and unconquerable will, those Caesars and Napoleons, whose footsteps shake the earth.

Waiting

We met at Waterloo; as we were paying the same visit, we travelled in the train together; but when we got out at that country station, she found that her boxes had not arrived. They might have gone on to the next station; I waited with her while enquiries were telephoned down the line. It was a mild spring evening: side by side we sat in silence on a wooden bench facing the platform; the bustle caused by the passing train ebbed away; the dusk deepened, and one by one the stars twinkled out in the serene sky.

'How peaceful it is!' I said. 'Is there not a certain charm,' I went on after another pause, 'in waiting like this in silence under the stars? It's after all a little adventure, isn't it? a mood with a colour and atmosphere of its own.'

'I often think,' I once more mused aloud, 'I often think that it is in moments like this of waiting and hushed suspense that one tastes most fully the savour of life, the uncertainty, and yet the sweetness of our frail mortal condition, so capable of fear and hope, so dependent on a million accidents.'

'Luggage!' I said, after another silence, 'isn't it after all absurd that Souls which voyage, thoughtfully, through strange seas should carry about with them brushes and drapery in leather boxes? Suppose all this paltry junk,' I said, giving my suit-case a poke with my umbrella, 'suppose all this junk should disappear, what after all would it matter?'

At last she spoke. 'But it's my luggage,' she said, 'which is lost.'

Ions

'Self-determination,' one of them insisted.

'Arbitration!' cried another.

'Co-operation?' suggested the mildest of the party.

'Confiscation!' answered an uncompromising female.

I, too, became slightly intoxicated by the sound of these vocables. And were they not the cure for all our ills?

'Inebriation!' I chimed in, 'Inundation, Afforestation, Flagellation, Transubstantiation, Co-education, Co-operation!'

The Wrong Word

We were talking of the Universe at tea, and one of our company declared that he at least was entirely without illusions. He had long since faced the fact that Nature had no sympathy with our hopes and fears, and was icily indifferent to our fate. The Universe, he said, was a great meaningless machine; Man, with his reason and moral judgements, was the product of blind forces, which, though they would so soon destroy him, he must yet despise. To endure this tragedy of our fate with passionless depair, never to wince or bow the head, to confront the hostile powers with high disdain, to fix with eyes of scorn the Gorgon face of

Destiny, to stand on the brink of the abyss, clenching his fist at the death-pale stars—this, he said, was his attitude, and it produced, as you can imagine, a powerful impression on the company. As for me, I was carried away completely.

'By Jove, that is a stunt!' I cried.

Becalmed

Half-way along the street I stopped; I had forgotten the errand which had brought me out. What was it I wanted? There was nothing on earth I wanted; I stood there, motionless, without desire, like a ship at sea, deserted of all winds. It seemed as if I might stand there for ever.

Then, as with the shadow of a cloud, or ripple of the returning breeze, the wind of impulse darkened over the waters and filled my sails again. Life was again momentous, full of meaning; and radiant to my imagination the stamps, red and green and golden, I had hurried out to buy.

A Slander

'But I'm told you don't believe in Love—'

'Now who on earth could have told you that?' I cried indignantly. 'Of course I believe in it;—there is no one more enthusiastic about Love than I am. I believe in it at all times and seasons, but especially in the Spring. Why, just think of it! True-love and the apple-blossoms, lovers who outwake the nightingales of April, the touch of hands and lips, and the clinging of flower-soft limbs together; and all this with, for a background, the gay, musical, perfumed landscape of the Spring. Why, nothing could be more genial, Miss Tomkins, more appropriate and pretty!

'Haven't I said so again and again, haven't I published it more than once in the weekly papers?'

Synthesis

'It's awful,' I said, 'I think it simply wicked, the way you tear your friends to pieces.'

'But you do it yourself, you know you do! You analyse and analyse people, and then you make them up again into creatures larger than life—'

'That's exactly it,' I answered gravely. 'If I take people to pieces, I do it so as to put them together again better than they were before; I make them more real, so to speak, more significant, more essentially themselves, if you catch my meaning. But to cut them up, as you do, and leave the fragments anyhow on the floor—I can't tell you how cruel and heartless and wrong I think it!'

Shrinkage

Sometimes my soul floats out beyond the constellations; then all the vast life of the Universe is mine. Then again it evaporates, it shrinks, it dwindles; and of that flood which over-brimmed the bowl of the great Cosmos there is hardly enough now left to fill a teaspoon.

Comfort

People often said that there was nothing sadder, She mourned, than the remembrance of past happiness; but to her it seemed that not the way we remember, but the way we forget, was the real tragedy of life. Everything fades from us; our joys and sorrows vanish alike in the irrevocable flux; we can't stay their fleeting. Didn't I feel, She moaned, the sadness of this forgetting, this outliving the things we care for; this constant dying, so to speak, in the midst of life?

I felt its sadness very much; I felt quite lugubrious about it. 'And yet,' I said (for I did really want to think of something that might console this lamentable lady), 'and yet can't we find, in this fading of recollection, some recompense, after all? Think, for instance—.' But what, alas, could I suggest?

'Think,' I began once more after a pause of deep consideration, 'think of forgetting, and reading, and reforgetting and re-reading all Jane Austen's novels!'

Ebury Street

'Do you mean to cut me? How odd you look! What are you doing in Ebury Street?' she asked.

I felt a large, healthy blush suffuse my features. 'There's a lady who lives here—no, I don't mean what you think—a lady,' I said desperately, 'a Mrs. Whigham, who hates the way I write, and threw my last book out of the window.

I walk by her house now and then to practise humility, and learn—as we all should learn—to endure the world's contempt.'

This Mrs. Whigham was, however, an invented being; I had really come to Ebury Street for another look, in the window of a shop there, at an old Venetian mirror, in whose depths of dusky glass I had seen a dim, romantic, well-dressed figure, as I went by one day.

The Welsh Harp

What charming corners one can find in the immense dinginess of London, and what curious encounters become a part of the London-lover's experience! The other day, when I walked beyond the Edgware Road, and stopped for tea at the Welsh Harp, on the banks of the Brent Reservoir, I found, behind the modern frontage of this inn, a garden adorned with sham ruins and statues, and full of autumn flowers and the shimmer of clear water. Sitting there and drinking my tea—alone, as I thought at first, in the twilight—I became aware that the garden had another occupant; that at another table, not far from me, a vague woman in a shabby bonnet was sitting, with her reticule lying by her, also drinking tea and gazing at the afterglow of the sunset. An elderly spinster I thought her, a dressmaker perhaps, or a retired governess, one of those maiden ladies who live alone in quiet lodgings, and are fond of romantic fiction and solitary excursions.

More than once, as we sat there, we two alone in the growing dusk, our glances met, and a curious relation of sympathy and understanding established itself between us; we seemed to carry on a dialogue full of tacit avowals. 'Yes,' we seemed to say, as our eyes met over our suspended tea-cups, 'yes, Beauty, Romance, the Blue Bird that sings of Happiness—these are the things we care for;—the only things that, in spite of everything, we still care for. But where can we find them in the dingy London streets?'

'And yet,' our eyes asked each other, 'isn't this garden, in its shabby, pretentious way, romantic; isn't it like something in a poem of Verlaine's; hasn't it now, in the dim light, a curious beauty? And this mood of meditation after our excellent tea, what name, if we are honest, can we call it by, if we don't call it Happiness?'

Misapprehension

People often seem to take me for someone else; they talk to me as if I were a person of earnest views and unalterable convictions. 'What is your opinion of Democracy?' they ask. 'Are you in favour of the Channel Tunnel?' 'Do you believe in existence after Death?'

I assume a thoughtful attitude, and by means of grave looks and evasive answers, I conceal—or at least I hope I conceal—my discreditable secret.

The Lift

What on earth had I come up for? I stood out of breath in my bedroom; I'd completely forgotten the errand which had carried me upstairs, leaping two steps at a time.

Gloves! Of course it was my gloves which I had left there. But what did gloves matter, I asked myself, in a world, bursting, as Dr. Johnson describes it, with Sin and Misery?

O stars and garters! how bored I am by this trite, moralizing way of regarding natural phenomena—this crying of vanity on the beautiful manifestations of nature's forces! This desire of mine to appear out of doors in appropriate apparel, if it can overcome gravitation; if it can shove twelve stone of matter thirty or forty feet above the earth's surface; if it can do this every day, and several times a day, isn't it quite as convenient in the house as a lift?

Sloane Street

When I walk out, middle-aged, but still sprightly, and still, if the truth must be told, with an idiot dream in my heart of some romantic encounter, I look at the passers-by, say in Sloane Street, and then I begin to imagine moon-faces more alluring than any I see in that thoroughfare. But then again vaster thoughts visit me, remote metaphysical musings; those faces like moons I imagined begin to wane as moons wane, the passers-by vanish; and immortal Reason, disdaining the daymoth she dwells with, turns away to her crystalline sphere of contemplation. I am lost out of Time; I walk on to Sloane Square in a world of white silence.

Regent's Park

I wondered, as I passed Regent's Park on my way to Hampstead, what kind of people live in those great stuccoed terraces and crescents, with their solemn façades and friezes and pediments and statues. People larger than life I picture the inhabitants of those august, unfashionable houses, people with a dignity of port, an amplitude of back, an emphasis of vocabulary and conviction unknown in other regions; Dowagers and Dignitaries who have retired from a world no longer worthy of them, ex-Governors of Dominions, unavailing Viceroys, superannuated Bishops and valetudinarian Generals, who wear top-hats and drive around the Park in old-fashioned barouches;— a society, I imagine it, not frivolous, not flippant, entirely devoid of double meanings; a society in which the memory of Queen Victoria is still revered, and regrets are still felt for the death of the Prince Consort.

Or, as I have sometimes fancied, are those commodious mansions the homes of the Victorian Statesmen and Royal Ladies and distinguished-looking Murderers who, in the nearby wax-work Exhibition, gaze on the shallow, modern generation which chatters and pushes all day before the glassy disapprobation of their eyes?

The Aviary

Peacock Vanities, great, crested Cockatoos of Glory, gay Infatuations and painted Daydreams;—what a pity it is all the Blue Birds of impossible Paradises have such beaks and sharp claws, that one really has to keep them shut up in their not too-cleanly cages!

St. John's Wood

As I walked on, the air soon lightened; the Throne, the Altar and the Top-Hat cast fainter shadows, the figures of John Bright and Gladstone and Queen Victoria evanesced, —they faded. I had entered the precincts of St. John's Wood; and as I went past its villas of coquettish aspect, with gay Swiss gables, with frivolously Gothic or Italian or almost Oriental faces, their lighter outlook on existence, the air they have of not taking life too earnestly, began to exert an influence.

St. John's Wood is the home in fiction of adventuresses and profligacy and outrageous supper-parties; often have I read about those foreign Countesses of unknown history and unbelievable fascination, who decoy handsome young officials of the Foreign Office to these villas, and rob them, in dim-lit, scented bedrooms, of important documents. But I at least have never too severely blamed these young diplomatists. Silent is the street as the mysterious brougham pauses, lovely the eyes that flash, and graceful the white-gloved hand that beckons from the carriage-window; and how can they resist (for they are only human) the lure of so adventurous, so enchanting an invitation?

The Garden Suburb

I had often heard of the Hampstead Garden Suburb, of the attempt of its inhabitants to create an atmosphere of the Higher Culture, to create, as it were, the Golden Age in that region. But I must now confess that it was in a spirit of profane curiosity that I walked up toward its courts and closes. And when I saw the notices of the Societies for Mothercraft and Handicraft and Child Study, the lectures on Reincarnation, the Holy Grail, and the Teaching of the Holy Zoroaster, I am afraid I laughed. But how thin this laughter sounded amid the quiet amenity, the beautiful distinction of this Utopia! It was an afternoon of daydreams; the autumnal light under the low clouds was propitious to inner recollection; and as I walked the streets of this transcendental city, soothed by the sense of order and beautiful architecture all around me, I began to feel that I too was an Idealist, that here was my spiritual home, and that it would be a seemly thing to give up the cinemas and come and make my abode on this hill-top. Pictures floated before my eyes of tranquil days, days of gardening and handicrafts and lectures, evenings spent in perusing the world's masterpieces.

Although I still frequent the cinemas, and spend too

much time gazing in at the windows of expensive shops, and the reverie of that afternoon has come to no fruition, yet I feel myself a better person for it: I feel that it marks me off from the merely cynical and worldly. For I at least have had a Pisgah sight of the Promised City; I have made its ideal my own, if but for an afternoon, and only in a daydream.

Sunday Calls

'Well, I must say!' Reason exclaimed, when we found ourselves in the street again.

'What's the matter now?' I asked uneasily.

'Why are you always trying to be someone else? Why not be what you really are?'

'But what am I really? Again I ask you!'

'I do hate to see you playing the ass; and think how they laugh at you!'

The glossy image of myself I had left in the house behind us began to tarnish.

'And what next?' my querulous companion went on. 'What will you be in South Kensington, I wonder? a sad, subtle, solitary Satan, disillusioned and distinguished; or a bluff, breezy sailor, fond of his bottle and boon companions?'

An Anomaly

When people embellish their conversation with a glitter of titles, and drag into it self-aggrandizing anecdotes, though I laugh at this peacock vein in them, I don't condemn it. Nay, since I too am human, since I too belong to the great household, would it be surprising if—say once or twice in my life—I also should have yielded to this tickling relish of the tongue?

No; but what is surprising is the way that I alone always escape detection: always throw dust in other people's eyes.

The Listener

The topic was one of my favourite topics, but I didn't at all feel on this occasion that it was I who was speaking. No, it was the Truth shining through me; the light of the Revelation which I had been chosen to blazon to the world. No wonder they were all impressed by my tones and gestures; no wonder even the fastidious lady whom it was most difficult to please kept watching me with an almost ecstatic attention.

As a cloud may obscure the sun in his glory, so from the morass of memory arose a tiny mist of words to darken my mind for a moment. I brushed them aside; they had no meaning. Sunning myself in the looking-glass of those eyes, never, for a moment, could I credit that devil-suggested explanation of their gaze.

Oh, no! that phrase I had heard, I had heard, the phrase, 'She mimics you to perfection,' was no more than a scrap of unintelligible jabber.

Caviare

'Aren't you ashamed of yourself?' asked my hostess, when she found me alone in the supper-room, after all the other guests had gone.

'Ashamed? Why should I be ashamed?' I asked, as I went on eating. 'I am simply following the precepts of Aristippus of Cyrene, who maintains that we should live wholly in the present moment, which alone exists, and in which alone the absolute Good of life is before us. It's only by regarding each Moment as an eternity, with no before or after, and by calmly and resolutely culling, without fear, or passion, or prejudice, the Good it offers—it is only thus, he says, that Wisdom is made manifest; only thus,' I explained, as I took another caviare-sandwich, 'that mortals can participate in the felicity of the Gods—the bright Gods, who feed on happiness for ever.'

Above the Clouds

'I do so hate gossip,' she murmured.

'How I hate it too!' I heard myself exclaim.

'There is so much that is good and noble in human nature; why not talk of that?'

'Why not indeed?' I sighed.

'I always feel that it is one's own fault if one dislikes people, or finds them boring.'

'How I agree with you!' I cried, as Virtue crept like a guilty thing into my heart.

'But people are nowadays so cynical—they sneer at everything that makes life worth living—Love, Faith, Friendship—'

'And yet those very names are so lovely that even when used in mockery they shine like stars.' (I should have died then; never again shall I be so fit for Heaven.)

'How beautifully you put it! I have so enjoyed our talk.' I had enjoyed it too, and felt all the better for it; only a little giddy and out of breath, as if I had been up in a balloon.

The Bubble

Walking home at night, troubled by the world's affairs, and with its weight of Wrong crushing down my poor shoulders, I sometimes allow my Soul an interlude of solace. From the jar in which I keep my Vanity bottled, I remove the cork; out rushes that friendly Jinn and swells up and fills the sky. I walk on transcendentally in another world, a world in which I cut a very different figure.

I shall not describe that exquisite, evanescent universe; I soon snuff it out, or it melts of itself in thin air.

Paradise Regained

The fields and old farm, the little river, the village church among elms, the formal gates of the park with the roofs of the Great House beyond, all made, in the evening air, a dream-like picture. I was strangely happy; and how familiar was every detail of the scene before me! There was the trout-stream I had fished in, there were the meadows I had galloped over;—through how many countless, quiet English years had I not lived here, and loved and hunted, courting innumerable vicars' daughters from cover to cover of all the countless, mild, old-fashioned novels of English country life which I have dreamed away my own life in reading?

Moments

'Awful moments? Why, yes, of course,' I said, 'life is full of them—let me think—'

'To find other people's unposted letters in an old pocket; to be seen looking at oneself in a street-mirror, or overheard talking of the Ideal to a Duchess; to refuse Nuns who come to the door to ask for subscriptions, or to be lent by a beautiful new acquaintance a book she has written full of mystical slip-slop, and dreadful musings in an old-world garden—'

Interruption

'Life,' said a gaunt widow, with a reputation for being clever—'life is a perpetual toothache.'

In this vein the conversation went on: the familiar topics were discussed of labour-troubles, epidemics, cancer, servants, and taxation.

Near me there sat a little old lady who was placidly drinking her tea, and taking no part in the melancholy chorus. 'Well, I must say,' she remarked, speaking in an undertone, 'I must say I enjoy life.'

'So do I,' I whispered.

'When I enjoy things,' she went on, 'I know it. Eating, for instance, the sunshine, my hot-water bottle at night. Other people are always thinking of unpleasant things.

'It makes a difference,' she added, as she got up to go with the others.

'All the difference in the world!' I answered.

Alchemy

It's too bad that I had no chance for a longer colloquy with this old Theban lady. I felt that we were congenial spirits, and had a lot to tell each other.

For she and I are not among those who fill the mind with garbage; we make a better use of that adorable endowment. We invite Thought to share, and by sharing to enhance, the pleasures of the delicate senses; we distil, as it were, an elixir from our goldenest moments, keeping out of the shining crucible of consciousness everything that tastes sour.

I do wish that we could have discussed at greater length, like two Alchemists, the theory and practice of our art.

The Ear-trumpet

They were talking of people I did not know. 'How do they spend their time there?' someone asked.

Then I, who had been sitting too long silent, lifted up my voice. 'Ah, that's a mysterious question, when you think of it, how people spend their time. We only see them after all in glimpses; but what, I often wonder, do they do in their hushed and shrouded hours—in all the mysterious interstices of their lives?'

'In the what?'

'In the times, I mean, when no one sees them. In the intervals.'

'But that isn't the word you used?'

'It's the same thing—the interstices—'

Of course there was a deaf lady present. 'What did you say?' she inquired, holding out her ear-trumpet for my answer.

Guilt

What should I think of? I asked myself as I opened my umbrella. How should I occupy my imagination that harsh, dusky, sloshy, winter afternoon, as I walked to Bedford Square? Should I think of Arabia; of Albatrosses, or of those great Condors who sleep on their outspread wings in the high white air above the Andes?

But a sense of guilt oppressed me. What had I done, or left undone? And the shadowy figures that seemed to menace and pursue me? Yes, I had wronged them; it was again those Polish Poets, it was Mickiewicz, Slowacki, Szymonowicz, Krasicki, Kochanowski;—and I'd never read one word of all their works!

Cadogan Gardens

Out of the fog a dim figure accosted me. 'I beg your pardon, Sir, but could you tell me how to get to Cadogan Gardens?'

'Cadogan Gardens? I am afraid I am lost myself. Perhaps, Sir,' I added (we two seemed oddly intimate in that white world of mystery together), 'perhaps, Sir, you can tell me where I can find the Gardens I'm looking for?' I breathed their name.

'Hesperian Gardens?' the voice repeated. 'I don't think I have ever heard of Hesperian Gardens.'

'Oh, surely!' I cried, 'that Garden of the Sunset and singing Maidens!'

The Rescue

As I sat there, hopeless, with my coat and hat on in my bedroom, I felt I had no hold on life, no longer the slightest interest in it. To gain all that the world can give I would not have raised a listless finger; and it was entirely without intention that I took a cigarette, and felt for matches in my pocket. It was the act of an automaton, of a corpse that twitches a little after life has left it.

But when I found that I hadn't any matches, that—hang it!—there wasn't a box of matches anywhere, then, with this vexation, life came flooding back—the warm, familiar sense of my own existence, with all its exasperation, all its charm.

The Epitaph

'But perhaps he is a friend of yours?' said my lips: 'Is it safe?' my eyes asked. 'Dare I tell you how awful I think him?'

It was safe; only silence fell upon them, those Sad Ones, who at my decease were to murmur, 'He never said an unkind word of anyone.'

'Alas, Farewell!' breathed, as it faded, that boyish day-dream of my Funeral.

The Popes of Rome

I love to lie in bed and read the lives of the Popes of Rome. I think I could read for ever the biographies of those Pontiffs. For while I am absorbed in the doings of one Innocent or Pius, the Pope before him fades away; the earlier Vicars of Christ have all vanished from my failing memory; I am ready to read anew, with ever-renewed amazement, the outrageous goings-on of those holy and obstinate old men.

Charm

'Speaking of Charm,' I said, 'there is one quality which I find very attractive, though most people don't notice it, and rather dislike it if they do. That quality is Observation. You read of it in eighteenth-century books—"a Man of much Observation," they say. So few people,' I went on, 'really notice anything—they live in theories and thin dreams, and look dully at you with investigating eyes. They take no real interest in the real world; but the Observers I speak of find it a source of inexhaustible fascination. Nothing escapes them; they can tell at once what the people they meet are like, where they belong, their profession, the kind of houses they live in. The slightest thing is enough for them to judge by—a tone of voice, a gesture, the way they put their hats on.'

'I always judge people,' one of the company remarked, 'by their shoes. It's people's feet I look at first. And shoe-laces now—what an awful lot shoe-laces can tell you!'

As I slipped my feet back under my chair, I subjected to a rapid reconsideration my notion of Charm.

The Concerto

'What a beautiful movement!' she murmured, as the music paused.

'Lovely!' I roused myself to echo, though I hadn't heard a note.

Immediately I found myself again in the dock; and again the trial began, that ever-recurring criminal Action in which I am both Judge and culprit, all the jury, and the advocate on either side.

I now pleaded my other respectable attainments and general good character; and then dropped back into my dream, letting the violins wail unheard through the other movements, and the Grand Piano tinkle.

Somewhere

Somewhere, far below the horizon, there is a City; some day I shall sail to find its harbour; by what star I shall steer, or where that seaport lies, I don't know; but somehow or other through calms and storms and the sea-noises I shall voyage, until at last some peak will arise, telling me I am near my destination; or I shall see, at dusk, a lighthouse, twinkling, momentarily, at its port.

The Miracle

After lighting the spirit-lamp in preparation for tea, she turned with her earnest eyes and gave me all her attention.

'But we have never had a real talk about serious things,' she said.

As she said it, I saw my danger; I was alone with that enthusiast, and she was going to talk to me about my Soul.

'Now help me, O ye Guardian Powers!' Thus did I invoke those more than mortal combatants who succour heroic minds in their worst extremities, aiding the pure Knight to defend his honour and life, and struggling Damsels to preserve that which is dearer to them than life itself.

Not too long was I forced to emulate those ladies; for, at the very crisis of my peril, the spirit-lamp flared up and almost exploded; the kettle was upset, and I found myself soon after in the safe street, with soul as inviolate as the unsullied mountain snow.

The Platitude

'It's after all the little things in life that really matter!'
I was as much chagrined as they were flabbergasted by
this involuntary outbreak; but I have become an expert in
that Taoist art of disintegration which Yen Hui described
to Confucius as 'the art of sitting and forgetting.' I have
learnt to lay aside my personality in embarrassed moments,
to dissolve this self of mine into the All Pervading; to fall
back, in fact, into the universal flux, and sit, as I now sat
there, a blameless lump of matter, rolled on according to
the heavens' rolling, with rocks and trees.

The Fetish

Enshrined in a box of white paste-board I keep upstairs
a black ceremonial object: it's my last link with Christen-
dom and grave Custom: only on sacred occasions does it
make its portentous appearance, only at some great tribal
dance of my race. To pageants of Woe I march with it, or
of the hugest Felicity: at great Hallelujahs of Wedlock, or
at last Valedictions, I hold it bare-headed as I bow before
altars and tombs.

Things to Say

'How did you get on with Mrs. Hearse? You didn't seem
to have much to say!'
'Have you ever noticed,' I asked, 'how, when you are

trying to talk to people, all sorts of inappropriate things to say float by with appealing faces?'

'With me,' I went on, 'these ghosts of the unspoken are sometimes platitudes; sometimes dreadful facts; or I am deafened, as I was just now, by wicked stories, which clamour like wild beasts behind the portcullis of my teeth.'

The Echo

Now and then, from the other end of the table, words and phrases reached us as we talked.

'What do they mean by Complexes?' she asked.

'Oh, it's only one of the catchwords of the day,' I answered. 'Everything's a Complex just now.'

'The talk of most people,' I went on, 'is simply—how shall I put it?—simply the ticking of clocks; it marks the hour, but it has no other interest. But I like to think for myself, to be something more than a mere mouthpiece—a mere sounding-board and echo of contemporary chatter.'

'Just listen!' I said, as again their voices reached our ears.

'It's simply one of the catchwords of the day,' someone was shouting, 'the merest echo of contemporary chatter!'

Routine

I live by the clock; all my activities, my exits and entrances, my times for smoking cigarettes and reading murder-stories, are synchronized and set in harmony with the earth's motion and the sun's. Much more than happiness

I love my habits, the timely routine and oscillation of the hours which carry me on through months and seasons. Thus my life spins silent on its axle; but at the least dislocation or jar—if the Post is late, or the Morning Paper doesn't turn up—I am giddy, I am undone; the ground rocks beneath my feet.

The Scavenger

'The parlour-maid and cook both gave notice—'

'My stomach is not at all what it should be—'

'Of course the telephone was out of order—'

'The coal they sent was all stones and coal-dust—'

'All the electric wiring has had to be renewed—'

'I find it impossible to digest potatoes—'

'My aunt has had to have eighteen of her teeth extracted—'

Am I nothing but a dust-bin or kitchen sink for other people's troubles?

Have I no agonies, no indigestions, no Aunts of my own?

The Hot-bed

It was too much; the news in the paper was appalling; Central Europe and the Continent of Asia in a state of chaos; no comfort anywhere; tempests in the Channel, earthquakes, famines, strikes, insurrections. The Burden of the Mystery, the weight of all this incorrigible world—was really more than I could cope with.

'To prepare a hot-bed for early vegetables, equal quantities are taken of horse-manure and fallen leaves; a large heap is built in alternate layers,' I read with passionate interest, 'of these materials; it is left for several days, and then turned over. The site of the hot-bed must be sheltered from cold winds, but open to the sunshine. Early and dwarf varieties of potatoes should be chosen; asparagus plants may be dug up from the open garden—'

Aphasia

'But you haven't spoken a word:—you ought to tell us what you think.'

'The truth is,' I whispered in her unaverted ear, 'the truth is, I talk too much. Think of all the years I have been wagging my tongue; think how I shall go on wagging it, till it's smothered in dust!'

'And the worst of it is,' I went on hoarsely whispering, 'the horror is that no one understands me; I can never make clear to anyone my view of things. I may talk till I am black in the face, and no one will ever know—I shall go down to the deep, dark grave—and no one will know what I mean.'

Mrs. Backe

Mrs. Backe would be down in a few minutes, so I waited in the drawing-room of this new acquaintance who had so kindly invited me to tea.

It is indiscreet, but I can't help it; if I am left alone in a room, I cannot help peering about at the ornaments and books. The habitations people make for their souls interest me like sea-shells, or the nests of birds.

'A lover of Switzerland,' I inferred, 'has travelled in the East—the complete works of Canon Farrar;—that big bust with whiskers is Mendelssohn, no doubt. Good heavens! a stuffed cat! And that Moorish plaque is rather awful. Still, many of the nicest people have no taste—'

Then I saw the clock—the pink china clock with the face of a monkey. Softly I stole from the room and downstairs, and closed the front-door behind me.

Magic

'Do you think there are Ghosts?' she foamed, her eyes ablaze, 'do you believe in Magic?'

'Are you interested in Etymology?' I asked. 'To my mind there is nothing more fascinating than the derivation of words;—I could spend my life just looking them up in the dictionary. That's the way to learn the wonder of real life and history. Think of *Magic,* for instance, it comes, as no doubt you know, from the Magi, or ancient priests of Persia.

'Don't you love our deposit of Persian words in English? To me they glitter like jewels in our northern speech. *Paradise,* for instance; and the names of flowers and gems and rich fruits and tissues—*Tulip* and *Lilac* and *Jasmin* and *Peach* and *Lapis Lazuli,'* I chanted, 'and *Azure* and *Taffeta* and *Scarlet.'*

116

Fame

Somewhat furtively I bowed in Knightsbridge to the new Moon; the little ceremony was no doubt a survival of prehistoric feelings, but the Wish that I breathed was an inheritance from a later epoch. It was an echo of Greece and Rome, the ideal ambition of their poets and heroes; the thought of it seemed to float through the air in starlight and music; I saw in a bright constellation those stately Immortals, their names rang in my ears.

'May I, too,—' I whispered, incredulously, lifting my hat to the Moon.

News-items

In spite of the delicacy of my moral feelings, and my unrelaxed solicitude for the maintenance of the right principles of conduct, I find I can read without tears of the retired Colonels who forge cheques, and the ladies of unexceptionable position who are caught pilfering furs in shops. Somehow the sudden lapses of respected people, odd indecorums, backbitings, bigamies, embezzlements, and attempted chastities—the surprising leaps they make now and then out of propriety into the police-courts—somehow news-items of this kind do not altogether—how shall I put it?—well, they don't absolutely blacken the sunshine for me.

And Clergymen? Well, if some Clergyman slips in, do not, inordinately, I pray you, gentle Reader, grieve on my account.

Whiskers

There was once a young man who thought he saw Life as it really is; who prided himself on looking at it grimly in the face without illusions. And he went on looking at it grimly, as he thought, for a good many years. This was his notion of himself; but one day, meeting some very young people, he saw, reflected as it were in their eyes, a bland old gentleman with a white waistcoat and Victorian whiskers, a lover of souls and sunsets, and noble solutions for all problems—

That's what he saw in the eyes of those atrocious young men.

The Spelling Lesson

The incident which had caused the laughter of those youngsters was not a thing to joke about. I expressed my conviction briefly; but the time-honoured word I made use of seemed unfamiliar to them;—they looked at each other and began whispering together. Then one of them asked in a hushed voice, 'It's *what,* did you say?'

I repeated my monosyllable loudly.

Again they whispered together, and again their spokesman came forward.

'Do you mind telling us how you spell it?'

'I spell it, I spell it with a W!', I shouted. 'W-R-O-N-G—WRONG!'

At the Club

'It's the result of Board School Education—'

'It's the popular Press—'

'It's the selfishness of the Working Classes—'

'It's the Cinema—'

'It's the Jews—'

'Paid Agitators!—'

'The decay of Faith—'

'The disintegration of Family Life—'

'I put it down,' I said, 'to Sun-Spots. If you want to know,' I went inexorably on, 'if you ask me the cause of all this modern Unrest—'

Delay

I was late for breakfast this morning, for I had been delayed in my heavenly hot bath by the thought of all the other Earnest Thinkers, who, at that very moment—I had good reason to believe it—were soaking the time away in hot baths all over London.

Smiles

When people smile to themselves in the street, when I see the face of an ugly man or uninteresting woman light up (faces, it would seem, not exactly made for happy smiling), I wonder from what visions within those smiles are reflected; from what footlights, what gay and incredible scenes, do they gleam of vain glory?

The Pear

'But everyone in Bloomsbury is enthusiastic about the book!' I protested.

'Well, what if they are?' was the answer.

I too am a Superior Person, but the predicament was awkward. To figure as the dupe of a vulgar admiration, to be caught crying stale fish at a choice luncheon party!

'Oh, of course!' I hit back, 'I know it's considered the thing just now to despise the taste of the age one lives in. No one, even in Balham, will admit that they have read the books of the day. But my attitude has always been' (what had it been? I had to think in a hurry) 'I have always felt that it was more interesting, after all, to belong to one's own epoch: to share its dated and unique vision, that flying glimpse of the great panorama which no subsequent generation can ever recapture. To be Elizabethan in the age of Elizabeth; romantic at the height of the Romantic Movement—'

But it was no good: I saw it was no good, so I took a large pear and ate it in silence.

I know a good deal about pears, and am particularly fond of them. This one was a *Doyenné du Comice,* the most delicious of all.

The Dawn

My imagination has its dancing-places, like the Dawn in Homer; there are terraces, with balustrades and marble fountains on them, where Ideal Beings smile as I draw near; there are ilex-groves and beech trees under which I hold forth for ever; gardens fairer than most earthly gardens where groups of ladies never grow weary of listening to my voice.

Insomnia

Sometimes, when I am cross and can't sleep, I engage in angry contests with the Opinions I object to. Into the room they flop, those bat-like monsters of Wrong-Belief and Darkness; and though they glare at me with the day-light faces of bullying talkers, and their voices are the voices that shout me down in argument, yet, in these noc-turnal controversies, it is always my assertions which admit no answer.

I don't spare them; it is now their turn to be lashed to fury; made to eat their words.

Reading Philosophy

'The abstractedness of the relation brings to conscious-ness no less strongly the foreignness of the Idea to natural phenomena. In its widest formulation—'; mechanically I turned the page, but what on earth was it all about? Some

Fancy must have been fluttering between my spectacles and book.

I turned and caught that pretty Daydream. To be a Wit —yes, while my eyes were reading Hegel, I had stolen out myself to amaze the world with my epigrams. Each conversation at its most breathless moment I had crowned with words of double meaning which had echoed all through Chelsea. Feared all my life-time for my repartees, when my ashes had been swept at last into an urn of moderate dimensions, I had still lived on the lips of men; still my plays on words had been laughed at, my sayings handed down in memoirs to ensuing ages.

Moral Triumph

When I see motors gliding up at night to great houses in the fashionable squares, I journey in them: I ascend the stairways of those palaces; and, ushered with éclat into drawing-rooms of splendour, I sun myself in the painted smiles of the Mayfair Jezebels, and in that world of rouge and diamonds, glitter like a star. There I quaff the elixir and sweet essence of mondain triumph, eating truffles to the sound of trumpets, and feasting at sunrise on lobster-salad and champagne.

But it's all dust, it's all emptiness and ashes. Ah! far away from there I retire into the desert to contend triumphantly with Demons; to overcome in holy combats unspeakable Temptations, and purify, by prodigious purges, my heart of base desire.

The Springs of Action

What am I? What is Man?

I had looked into lots of books for an answer to this problem, before I came on Jeremy Bentham's simple and satisfactory solution: Man is a mechanism, moved by just so many springs of Action. These springs he enumerates in elaborate tables; and glancing over them this morning before getting up, I began with *Charity, All-embracing Benevolence, Love of Knowledge, Laudable Ambition, Godly Zeal.* Then I waited, but there was no buzz of any wheel beginning to move in my inner mechanism. I looked again: I saw *Arrogance, Ostentation, Vainglory, Abomination, Rage, Fury, Revenge;* and I was about to leap out of bed in a paroxysm of dreadful passions, when fortunately my eye fell on another set of motives: *Love of Ease, Indolence, Procrastination, Sloth.*

In the Cage

'What I say is, what I say!' I vociferate, as—a Parrot in the great cage of the World—I hop ostentatiously screeching, 'What I say is!' from perch to perch.

Voices

'You smoke too much!' whispers the still small voice of Conscience.

'You are a failure, nobody likes you,' Self-contempt keeps muttering.

'What's the good of it all?' sighs Disillusion, arid as a breath from the Sahara.

I can't tell you how these Voices bore me; but I can listen all day with grave attention to that suave bosom-Jesuit who keeps on unweariedly proving how all my acts and appetites and inclinations are in the most amazing harmony with the dictates of the Moral Law.

Complacency

Dove-grey and harmless as a dove, full of piety and innocence and pure thoughts, my Soul brooded unaffectedly within me;—I was only half listening to the shrill voice of Lady Screech. And I began to wonder, as more than once in little moments like this I have wondered, whether I might not be something more, after all, than a mere echo or compilation—could not claim, in fact, to possess a personality of my own.

Might it not be worth while, I now asked myself, to follow up this pleasing conjecture; to retire like Descartes from the world, and spend the rest of life, as he spent it, trying to prove my own existence?

The Rationalist

Occultisms, incantations, glimpses of the Beyond, intimations from another world—all kinds of supernaturalisms are most distasteful to me; I cling to the known world of explicable phenomena; and I was much put out to find this morning a cabalistic inscription written in letters of large menace on my bathroom floor. TAM HTAꓭ—what could be the meaning of these awful words, and how on earth had they got there? Like Belshazzar, my thoughts were troubled by this writing, and my knees smote one against the other; till majestic Reason, deigning to look downward from her contemplation of eternal causes, spelt backwards for me, with a pitying smile, the inscription on the BATH MAT, which was lying there, wrong side up.

Phrases

Is there, after all, any solace like the solace and consolation of Language? When I am disconcerted by the unpleasing aspects of existence, when to me, as to Hamlet, this earth seems a sterile promontory, it is not in Metaphysics nor in Religion that I seek for reassurance, but in fine phrases. The thought of gazing on life's Evening Star makes of ugly old age a pleasing prospect; if I call Death mighty and unpersuaded, it has no terrors for me; I am perfectly content to be cut down as a flower, to flee as a shadow, to be swallowed like a snowflake on the sea. These similes soothe and effectually console me. I am sad only at the thought that Words must perish like all things mortal; that the most perfect Metaphors must be forgotten when the human race is dust.

'But the iniquity of Oblivion blindly scattereth her Poppy.'

Athanasius

Since I have reason to believe that the age I live in is not an Age of Gold, and am quite disenchanted of all hope that the earth will turn to Paradise at present, I have intermitted the superintendence of public occurrences, and given over the helm and pilotage of the Ship of State to other hands. Concerned no longer with the fate of the Empire and the Universe, and quite undistracted by the supposed onrush of all things to darkness and the dogs, I sit at home and moon over the qualities of certain little books like this one—little elixirs of perfection, full of subtlety and sadness—which I can read and read again.

Although my taste in letters is by now, I must believe, almost absolutely flawless, yet conceivably, in some minute particulars, I may polish and improve it; that thus—zealous, like all the elect to narrow the privilege of Salvation—I may promulgate, and if necessary maintain alone against the world, an Athanasian creed of literary judgements, which whosoever shall not keep pure and undefiled, without doubt he shall perish everlastingly.

Ask Me No More

Where are the snows of yesteryear? Ask me no more the fate of Roses, or of Nightingales, or where the old Moons go, or what becomes of last year's Oxford poets.

Joy

Sometimes at breakfast, sometimes in a train or empty bus, or on the moving stairs at Charing Cross, I am happy; the earth turns to gold, and life becomes a magical adventure. Only yesterday, travelling alone to Sussex, I became light-headed with this sudden joy. The train seemed to rush to its adorable destination through a world newborn in brightness, bathed in a beautiful element, fresh and clear as on the morning of Creation. Even the coloured photographs of South Coast watering-places in the railway carriage shone with the light of Paradise upon them. Brighton faced me; next to it divine Southsea beckoned; and oh, the esplanade at Ryde! Then I saw the beach at Sidmouth, the Tilly Whim caves near Swanage;—was it in those un-haunted caves, or amid the tumult of life which hums about the Worthing bandstand, that I should find Bliss in its quintessence?

Or on the pier at St. Peter Port perhaps, in the Channel Islands, amid that crowd who watch in eternal ecstasy the ever-arriving, never-disembarking Weymouth steamer?

In Arcady

When I retire from London to my rural solitudes, and taste once more, as always, those pure delights of Nature which the Poets celebrate—walks in the unambitious meadows, and the ever-satisfying companionship of vegetables and flowers—I am nevertheless haunted now and then (but tell it not to Shelley's Skylark, nor whisper to Wordsworth's Daffodils, the disconcerting secret)—I am incongruously beset by longings of which the Lake Poets never sang. Echoes and images of the abandoned City discompose my arcadizings; I hear, in the babbling of brooks, the atrocious sound of London gossip, and newsboys' voices in the cries of birds. Sometimes the gold-splashed distance of a country lane seems to gleam at sunset with the posters of the evening papers; I dream at dawn of dinner-invitations, when like a telephone-call, I hear the Greenfinch trill his electric bell.

Worries

In the woods about my garden and familiar precincts lurk the fears of life; all threaten me, some I may escape, of others I am the destined and devoted victim. Sooner or later—and yet in any case how soon!—I shall fall, as I have seen others fall, touched by an unseen hand.

But I do not think of these Terrors often, though I seem to hear them sometimes moving in the thickets. It is the little transitory worries that bite and annoy me, querulous insects, born of the moment, and perishing with the day.

Property

It's endorsed by Society, defended by the Church, maintained by the Law, and the slightest tamperings with private property are severely punished by elderly Judges in large horsehair wigs. Oh, certainly it must be all right; *I have a feeling that it is all right;* and one of these days I shall get someone to explain why the world keeps on putting adequate sums of its currency into my pocket.

But of course it's all right—

Mrs. Braye

'Mrs. Braye is so sorry she couldn't come. She longs to see your garden; but she is shut up with an awful cold.'

'Thank God!' I exclaimed.

'But I thought you liked Mrs. Braye?'

'Indeed I do—I do like her immensely! Who could help liking her? her generous nature, her gift for appreciation, her whole-hearted, fervid enthusiasm?

'It's only that I am afraid—I am awfully afraid, to tell you the truth—of her adjectives.'

The Danger of Going to Church

As I came away from the Evening Service, walking home from that Sabbath adventure, some neighbours of mine met and passed me in their motor, laughing. Were they laughing at me? I wondered uneasily; and as I sauntered across the fields I vaguely cursed those misbelievers. Yes, yes, their eyes should be darkened, and their mocking lips put to silence. They should be smitten with the botch of Egypt, and a sore botch in the legs that cannot be healed. All the teeth should be broken in the mouths of those bloody men and daughters of backsliding; their faces should become as flames, and their heads be made utterly bald. Their little ones should be dashed to pieces before their eyes, and brimstone scattered upon their habitations. They should be led away with their buttocks uncovered; they should stagger to and fro as a drunken man staggereth in his vomit.

But as for the Godly Man who kept his Sabbaths, his should be the blessings of those who walk in the right way. 'These blessings'—the words came back to me from the Evening Lesson—'these blessings shall come upon thee, and overtake thee.' And suddenly, in the mild summer air, it seemed as if, like a swarm of bees inadvertently wakened, the blessings of the Old Testament were actually rushing after me. From the hot, remote, passionate past of Hebrew history, out of the Oriental climate and unctuous lives of that infuriate people, gross good things were coming to overwhelm me with Benedictions for which I had not bargained. Great oxen and camels and concubines were panting close behind me, he-goats and she-goats and rams of the breed of Bashan. My barns should burst their doors with plenty, and all my paths drop fatness. My face should be smeared with the oil of rejoicing; all my household and the beasts of my household should beget and bear increase; and as for the fruit of my own loins, it should be for multitude as the sands of the sea, and as the stars of heaven. My little ones should be as olive plants about my table; sons and daughters, and their sons and daughters to the third and fourth generation, should rise up and call me blessed.

My feet should be dipped in butter; I should sit under my fig-tree with my heel on the neck of my enemy, and my eyes stand out with fatness; I should flourish as the Cedar of Lebanon that bringeth forth fruit in old age.

Things to Write

What things there are to write, if one could only write them! My mind is full of gleaming thoughts; gay moods and mysterious, moth-like meditations hover in my imagination, fanning their painted wings. They would make my fortune if I could catch them; but always the rarest, those freaked with azure and the deepest crimson, flutter away beyond my reach.

The ever-baffled chase of these filmy nothings often seems, for one of sober years in a sad world, a trifling occupation. But have I not read of the great Kings of Persia who used to ride out to hawk for butterflies, nor deemed this pastime beneath their royal dignity?

The Vicar of Lynch

When I heard through country gossip of the strange happening at Lynch which had caused so great a scandal, and had led to the disappearance of the deaf old Vicar of that remote village, I collected all the reports I could about it, for I felt that at the centre of this uncomprehending talk and wild anecdote, there was something with more meaning than a mere sudden outbreak of blasphemy and madness.

It appeared that the old Vicar, after some years spent in the quiet discharge of his parochial duties, had been noticed to become more and more odd in his appearance and behaviour; and it was also said that he had gradually introduced certain alterations into the Church services. These had been vaguely supposed at the time to be of a High Church character, but afterward they were put down to a growing mental derangement, which had finally culminated at that infamous Harvest Festival, when his career as a clergyman of the Church of England had ended. On this painful occasion the old man had come into church outlandishly dressed, and had gone through a service with chanted gibberish and unaccustomed gestures, and prayers which were unfamiliar to his congregation. There was also talk of a woman's figure on the altar, which the Vicar had unveiled at a solemn moment in this performance; and I also heard echo of other gossip—gossip that was, however, authoritatively contradicted and suppressed as much as possible—about the use of certain other symbols of a most unsuitable kind. Then a few days after the old man had disappeared—some of the neighbours believed that he was dead; some, that he was now shut up in an asylum for the insane.

Such was the fantastic and almost incredible talk I listened to, but in which, as I say, I found more meaning than my neighbours. For one thing, although they knew that the Vicar had come from Oxford to this remote College living, they knew nothing of his work and scholarly reputation in that University, and none of them had probably ever heard of—much less read—an important book which he had written, and which was the standard work on his special subject. To them he was simply a deaf, eccentric, and solitary clergyman; and I think I was the only person in the neighbourhood who had conversed with him on the subject concerning which he was the greatest living authority in England.

For I had seen the old man once—curiously enough at the time of a Harvest Festival, though it was some years before the one which had led to his disappearance. Bicycling one day over the hills, I had ridden down into a valley of cornfields, and then, passing along an unfenced road that ran across a wide expanse of stubble, I came, after getting off to open three or four gates, upon a group of thatched cottages, with a little, unrestored Norman church standing among great elms. I left my bicycle and walked through the churchyard, and as I went into the church, through its deeply-recessed Norman doorway, a surprisingly pretty sight met my eyes. The dim, cool, little interior was set out and richly adorned with an abundance of fruit and vegetables, yellow gourds, apples and plums and golden wheat-sheaves, great loaves of bread, and garlands of September flowers. A shabby-looking old clergyman was standing on the top of a step-ladder, finishing the decorations, when I entered. As soon as he saw me he came down, and I spoke to him, praising the decorations, and raising my voice a little, for I noticed that he was deaf. We spoke of

133

the Harvest Festival; and as I soon perceived that I was talking with a man of books and University education, I ventured to hint at what had vividly impressed me in that old, gaudily-decorated church—its pagan character, as if it were a rude archaic temple in some corner of the antique world, which had been adorned, two thousand years ago, by pious country folk for some local festival. The old clergyman was not in the least shocked by my remark; it seemed indeed rather to please him; there was, he agreed, something of a pagan character in the modern Harvest Festival—it was no doubt a bit of the old primitive Vegetation Ritual, the old Religion of the soil; a Festival which, like so many others, had not been destroyed by Christianity, but absorbed into it, and given a new meaning. 'Indeed,' he added, talking on as if the subject interested him, and expressing himself with a certain donnish carefulness of speech that I found pleasant to listen to, 'the Harvest Festival is undoubtedly a survival of the prehistoric worship of that Corn Goddess who, in classical times, was called Demeter and Ioulo and Ceres, but whose cult as an Earth-Mother and Corn-Spirit is of much greater antiquity. For there is no doubt that this Vegetation Spirit has been worshipped from the earliest times by agricultural peoples; the wheat fields and ripe harvest being naturally suggestive of the presence amid the corn of a kindly Being, who, in return for due rites and offerings, will vouchsafe nourishing rains and golden harvests.' He mentioned the references in Virgil, and the description in Theocritus of a Sicilian Harvest Festival—these were no doubt familiar to me; but if I was interested in the subject, I should find, he said, much more information collected in a book which he had written, but of which I had probably never heard, about the Vegetation Deities in Greek Religion. I knew the book, and felt now much interested in my chance meeting with its author; and after expressing this as best I could, I rode off, promising to visit him again. This promise I was never able to fulfil; but when afterward, on my return to the neighbourhood, I heard of that unhappy scandal, my memory of this meeting and our talk enabled me to form a theory as to what had really happened.

It seemed plain to me that the change had been too violent for this elderly student, taken from his books and college rooms and set down in the solitude of this remote valley, amid the richness and living sap of Nature. The gay spectacle, right under his old eyes, of growing shoots and budding foliage, of blossoming and flowering, and the ripening of fruits and crops, the pairing of birds and the mating of cattle, had little by little (such was my theory) unhinged his brains. More and more his thoughts had come to dwell, not on the doctrines of the Church in which he had long ago taken orders, but on the pagan rites which had formed his life-long study, and which had been the expression of ways not unlike the agricultural life amid which he now found himself living. So as his derangement grew upon him in his isolation, he had gradually transformed, with a holy cunning, the Christian services, and led his little congregation, all unknown to themselves, back toward their ancestral worship of the Corn-Goddess. At last he had thrown away all disguise, and had appeared as a hierophant of Demeter, dressed in a fawn skin, with a crown of poplar leaves, and pedantically carrying the mystic basket and the winnowing fan appropriate to these mysteries. The wheaten posset he offered the shocked communicants belonged to these also, and the figure of a woman on the altar was of course the holy Wheatsheaf, whose unveiling was the culminating point in that famous ritual.

It is much to be regretted that I could not recover full and more exact details of that celebration, in which this great scholar had probably embodied his mature knowledge concerning a subject which has puzzled generations of students. But what powers of careful observation could one expect from a group of labourers and small farmers? Some of the things that reached my ears I refused to believe—the mention of pig's blood, for instance, and especially the talk of certain ithyphallic symbols, which the choir boys, it was whispered, had carried in their hands about the church in ceremonious procession. Village people have strange imaginations; and to this event, growing more and more monstrous as they talked it over, they must themselves have added this grotesque detail. However, I have written to consult an Oxford authority on this interesting point, and he has been kind enough to explain at length that although at the *Haloa,* or winter festival of the Corn-Goddess, and also at the *Chloeia,* or festival in early spring, some symbolization of the reproductive powers of Nature would be proper and appropriate, such ritualism would have been quite out of place at the *Thalysia,* or autumn festival of thanksgiving. I feel certain that a solecism of this kind—the introduction into a particular rite of features not sanctioned by the texts—would have seemed a shocking thing to one who had always been so accurate a scholar.

In a Fix

To go, or not to go? Did I want or not want to bicycle over to the Hanbury-Belchers' at Pokemore? Wouldn't it be pleasanter to stay at home?

I liked the Hanbury-Belchers—

Or did I really like them?

Still, it might be pleasant?

But how beforehand can one ever tell? Experience? I was still, I felt, as ignorant of life as a newborn infant; experience has taught me nothing; what I needed was some definite, a priori principle, some clear conception of the meaning of existence, in the light of which problems of this kind would solve themselves at once.

I leant my bicycle against the gate, and sat down to think the matter out. Calling to mind the moral debates of the old philosophers, I meditated on that *Summum Bonum,* or Sovereign Felicity of which they argued; but from their disputes and cogitations what came back most vividly— what seemed to fall upon me almost in a hush of terror— was that paralysis or dread balance of desire which they wrote of; the predicament, in fact, of that philosophic unguinulate, who, because he found in each of them pre-

cisely the same attraction, stood between two bundles of
hay, unable to move, until he perished of hunger.

The Garden Party

'Yes, I suppose it is rather a dull Garden Party,' I agreed,
though my local pride was a little hurt by the disdain of
that visiting young woman for our rural society. 'Still we
have some interesting neighbours, when you get to know
them. Now that fat lady over there in purple—do you see
her? Mrs. Turnbull—she believes in Eternal Torment.
And that old gentleman with whiskers and white spats,
Colonel Bosco, is convinced that England is tottering on
the very brink of the Abyss. He expects to hear at any moment the final crash of Empire, Church, and Throne; and
it gives him, he says, a kind of giddy feeling. And the pie-
faced lady he is talking to, Miss Stuart-Frisby, was, she
tells us, Mary Queen of Scots in a previous existence. And
our Curate—we're proud of our Curate, he's a great crick-
eter, and a kind of saint as well. They say he goes out in
Winter at three o'clock in the morning, and stands up to
his neck in a pond, to cool and overcome his appetites.'

Weltschmerz

'How depressed you look! What on earth's the matter?'
'Central Europe,' I said, 'and the chaos in China is some-
thing awful. There's a threatened shortage, too, of beer in
Copenhagen.'

138

'But why should that worry you?'

'It doesn't. It's what I said to Mrs. Rumbal—I do say such idiotic things! She asked me to come to see them. "I shall be delighted," I said, "as delighted—"'

'But it's your fault for making me read that book of Siamese translations!'—

'"As delighted," I said, "Mrs. Rumbal, as a royal flamingo, when he alights upon a cluster of lotuses."'

Life-enhancement

I was simply telling them at tea the details of my journey—how late the train had been in starting, how crowded the railway carriage, how I had mislaid my umbrella, and nearly lost my Gladstone bag.

But how I enjoyed making them listen, what a sense of enhanced existence I found it gave me (and to think that I have pitied bores!) to force my doings, my interests, my bag and umbrella, down their throats!

The Pyramid

'To read Gibbon,' I said, as we paced that terrace in the sunshine, 'to peruse his metallic, melancholy pages, and then forget them; to re-read and re-forget the *Decline and Fall;* to fill the mind with that great, sad, splendid, meaningless panorama of History, and then to watch those Kings and Conquerors, those Heresiarchs and monks and

Patriarchs and Councils, all fade away from our memory, as they have faded from the glass of Time—'

As she turned to me with a glance full of enthusiasm, 'What is so enchanting,' I reflected, 'as the dawn of an acquaintance with a clever woman with whom one can share one's thoughts?'

It was her remark about History, how she believed that the builders of the Great Pyramid had foreseen and fore-told many events of Modern History, which made a soul-estranging shadow, an Egyptian darkness, loom between us on that terrace.

Eclipse

A mild radiance and the scent of flowers filled the draw-ing-room, whose windows stood open to the summer night. I thought our talk delightful; the topic was one of my favourite topics; I had much that was illuminating to say about it, and I was a little put out when we were called to the window to look at the planet Jupiter, which was shining in the sky just then, we were told, with great bril-liance.

In turns through a telescope we gazed at the Planet. I thought the spectacle over-rated. However I said nothing. Not for the world, not for any number of worlds would I have wished them to guess why I was not pleased with that Star.

Reflections

When I walk to the side of the thought-suggesting sea, when I sit on the sand not far from the margin of the incoming or retreating tide, I often gaze on that waste of undulating water until it assumes in my eyes a moral meaning—seems to lie there on the page of Nature's book as an immense and shining metaphor, re-presenting the instability and transience of all things in the stream of Time. And the waves, as they hasten towards the pebbled shore, remind me, as they have reminded others, of our own moments hastening to their end.

But as they keep on reiterating monotonously the lesson, and my thoughts ebb and flow to their melancholy music, they seem to efface and wash away their own monitions: my sense of the transience of things proves itself but a transient reflection; and reclining there in the shade of my white cotton sun-umbrella, I float agreeably off into an oblivion of Time, the Sea, and Mortality.

The Ideal

Bright shone the morning, and as I waited (they had promised to call for me in their motor) I made for myself an enchanting picture of the day before me, our drive to that forest beyond the dove-blue hills, the ideal beings I should meet there, feasting with them exquisitely in the shade of immemorial trees.

And when, in the rainy twilight, I was deposited, soaked,

and half-dead with fatigue, out of that open motor, was there nothing inside me but chill and disillusion? If I had dreamed a dream incompatible with the climate and social conditions of these Islands, had I not, out of that very dream and disenchantment, created, like the Platonic Lover, a Platonic and imperishable vision—the ideal Picnic, the Picnic as it might be—the wonderful windless weather, the Watteauish landscape, where a group of mortals talk and feast as they talked and feasted in the Golden Age?

Bogeys

I remember how charmed I was with these new acquaintances, to whose house I had been taken that afternoon to call. I remember the gardens through which we sauntered, with peaches ripening on the sunny walls; I remember the mellow light on the old portraits in the drawing-room, the friendly atmosphere and tranquil voices; and how, as the quiet stream of talk flowed on, one subject after another was pleasantly mirrored on its surface;—till, suddenly, at a chance remark, there was a sudden change and darkening, an angry swirl, as if a monster had splashed its head above the waters.

What was it about, the disputation into which we plunged, in spite of our desperate efforts to clutch at other subjects? Was it Tariff Reform or Table-rapping—Bacon and Shakespeare, Disestablishment, perhaps—or Anti-Vivisection? What did any of us know or really care about it? What force, what fury drove us into saying the stupid, intolerant, denunciatory things we said; that made us feel we would rather die than not say them? How could a group of polite and intelligent people be so suddenly transformed into barking animals?

Why do we let these Abstractions and implacable Dogmatisms take possession of us, glare at each other through our eyes, and fight their futile, frenzied conflicts in our persons? Life without the rancours and ever-recurring battles of these Bogeys might be so simple, friendly, affectionate, and pleasant!

Weltanschauung

When, now and then, on a calm night I look up at the Stars, I reflect on the wonders of Creation, the unimportance of this Planet, and the possible existence of other worlds like ours. Sometimes the self-poised and passionless shining of those serene orbs is what I think of; sometimes Kant's phrase comes into my mind about the majesty of the Starry Heavens and the Moral Law; or I remember Xenophanes gazing up at the broad firmament, and crying, 'The All is One!' and thus, in that sublime assertion, enunciating for the first time the great doctrine of the Unity of Being.

But these Thoughts are not my thoughts; they eddy through my mind like scraps of old paper, or withered leaves in the wind. What I really feel is the survival of a much more primitive mood—a view of the world which dates indeed from before the invention of language. It has never been put into literature; no poet has sung of it, no historian of human thought has so much as alluded to it; astronomers in their glazed observatories, with their eyes glued to the ends of telescopes, seem to have had no notion of it.

But sometimes, far off at night, I have heard a dog howling at the Moon.

The Alien

The older I grow, the more of an alien I find myself in the world; I cannot get used to it, cannot believe that it is real. I think I must have been made to live on some other Star. Or perhaps I am subject to hallucinations and hear voices; perhaps what I seem to see is delusion and doesn't happen; perhaps people don't really say the things I think I hear them saying.

Ah, someone ought to have told me when I was young, I should certainly have been told of the songs that are sung in drawing-rooms; they ought to have warned me about the fat women who suddenly get up and bellow out incredible recitations.

Achievement

'Yes, as you say, one certainly ought to try to make something of one's life. It's an experience after all, full of exasperation of course, but full of interest. And making love, and the warmth of the sun are pleasant, and money, and the taste of food. And how pleasant it is, too, to shine in conversation!'

'What I think would be perfectly charming,' I confided to our Vicar's wife, 'what above all things I should like, would be to make out of my life—how shall I put it?—something delicate and durable, something privileged to win the approbation of the high authorities of the Universe. To live on, in fact, after my funeral in a perfect phrase.'

AFTERTHOUGHTS

'Little fish are sweet'

AFTERTHOUGHTS

I. Life and Human Nature

We're the children of our age, but children who can never know their mother.

It is just as well to be a little giddy-pated, if you're to feel at home on this turning earth.

The future looms a dark fog before us; but through it we see the eyes of Posterity, gazing at us coldly.

How furious it makes people to tell them of the things which belong to their peace!

All mirrors are magical mirrors; never can we see our faces in them.

Our lives within may be mysteries and marvels; but our names and noses are too familiar to the world.

There are two things to aim at in life: first, to get what you want; and, after that, to enjoy it. Only the wisest of mankind achieve the second.

Happiness is a wine of the rarest vintage, and seems insipid to a vulgar taste.

That amusing stories are told about us doesn't amuse the Soul.

How awful to reflect that what people say of us is true!

Our names are labels, plainly printed on the bottled essense of our past behaviour.

As oysters secrete scale by scale the shells which overcrust their pearly seclusion, so our souls exude act by act the rough personage which hides quietly away from the world our irrelevant dream of existence.

My festival is a festival of Imagination on the way to the palace.

How exquisitely ironic is the entertainment we can derive from our disillusions!

For souls in growth, great quarrels are great emancipations.

The actual is egregious and disconcerting, and never more so than when the Ideal becomes real, and Heaven touches earth for the moment.

How many of our daydreams would darken into nightmares, were there a danger of their coming true!

What happens is mere litter; but from this wastepaper of perishable events Thought can unpack imperishable meanings.

Amid the vast unimportance of all things, how beyond all calculation important we find it each morning to have at hand, as we sit facing Time and Eternity, an adequate supply of thin paper!

Solvency is entirely a matter of temperament.

All-glorious within us are our gay pretensions; but when they fly from our lips, how are their wings bereft of their glory!

That we should practise what we preach is generally admitted; but anyone who preaches what he and his hearers practise must incur the gravest moral disapprobation.

It is only those who can declare without guile that they are doing the very opposite of what they are really doing—meat-eating vegetarians for instance, and snob-hating snobs—who keep stainless their serene ideals, and walk the earth in white, like angels.

Self-respecting people don't care to peep at their reflections in unexpected mirrors.

Are we all alike, all pleased alike and troubled by that wanton Eye so reprobated by the Founder of our Faith?

Only those who get into scrapes with their eyes open can find the safe way out.

The lusts of the Body scandalize the Soul; but it has to come to heel.

We are told by Moralists with the plainest faces that immorality will spoil our looks.

Money and sex are forces too unruly for our reason; they can only be controlled by taboos which we tamper with at our peril.

If you eradicate a fault, you leave room for a worse fault to take root and flourish.

There are few sorrows, however poignant, in which a good income is of no avail.

What is more mortifying than to feel you've missed the Plum for want of courage to shake the Tree?

Great felicities are often the great Misfortunes.

Little superstitions are spiders of the mind. Look out! Brush 'em away, or they'll choke it.

We need bogeys and awful apprehensions to keep us from getting dull.

'On the hill at Bomma, at the mouth of the Congo River,' Frazer tells us, in a sentence which seems to solve all the problems, 'dwells Namvulu Vulu, king of the rain and storm.'

Sound is more than sense.

That we are all lost in a world of vain illusion; and that somewhere, somehow, we must all seek Salvation and a more Abiding City—this is what old-fashioned parsons keep droning from their pulpits. The worst of it is, what they say is true.

'Seven great poplars, and amid those poplars, a golden well.'

It is through the cracks in our brains that ecstasy creeps in.

An echo of music, a face in the street, the wafer of the new moon, a wanton thought;—only in the iridescence of things the vagabond Soul is happy.

An act of folly isn't foolish, when you know it for the folly it is.

Look at the Moon! You may not know it, but there is something wrong about the Moon. She won't keep her appointments, nor stick to the programme laid down for her by the lunar theorists. At the end of the nineteenth century she got there ten seconds late: was fourteen seconds ahead of time a hundred years before.

There are tens of thousands, we are told, who are capable of achieving success in the ordinary walks of life; hundreds there are who can rule their fellow-men and wield empires, to one who can even understand the problem presented by the retardations and accelerations of this incalculable orb. But even these aristocrats of the intellect, ranking, we are told, above all other aristocracies in the scale of being, and including Ernest W. Brown and G. W. Hill among their most illustrious members, have never been able to calculate the motion of the Moon: still she laughs at their attempts to account for her lunacy.

II. Age and Death

It seemed so simple when one was young, and new ideas were mentioned, not to grow red in the face and gobble!

But we are forced like the insects, and can't help it, to undergo all the metamorphoses preordained for our species.

154

We grow with years more fragile in body, but morally stouter, and can throw off the chill of a bad conscience almost at once.

An evil name—a drawback at first—sheds lustre on old age.

There are people who, like houses, are beautiful in dilapidation.

What's more enchanting than the voices of young people, when you can't hear what they say?

Don't laugh at a youth for his affectations; he's only trying on one face after another till he finds his own.

Youth is at war with Time; but why should a youth of high fancy quarrel with that Abstraction which ripens his talent, and mellows his portrait with the varnish of years?

If we shake hands with icy fingers, it is because we have burnt them so horribly before.

Just when they sit down to enjoy in peace their evening meal of existence, the tables of most parents are pounced upon as by harpies, and pillaged by their children.

Parents used to care more for their money than their family; now they have to pay for their children's friendship through the nose.

The fiery thought of a social slip which makes us feel hot all over, will mellow into a glow to warm our aging bones.

I can't forgive my friends for dying; I do not find these vanishing acts of theirs at all amusing.

We all do ugly things, but our last great act is the ugliest of all.

Why are happy people not afraid of Death, while the insatiable and the unhappy so abhor that grim Feature?

III. Other People

There are men and women born into the world to do its work and win its prizes; others, simply to look on and see what happens. These two kinds of people feel ashamed when they meet each other.

It's an odd thing about this Universe that though we all disagree with each other, we are all of us always in the right.

If with an excess of interest you peer into the lives of other people, what you will probably find is that you have to pay their debts.

Those who set out to serve both God and Mammon soon discover that there is no God.

The word Snob belongs to the sour-grape vocabulary.

There are people I know such horrid things about, that I feel ashamed of myself when I meet them in drawing-rooms, making a good impression.

When we say we are certain so-and-so can't possibly have done it, what we mean is that we think he very likely did.

If we disregard what the world says of someone, we live to repent it.

The World is not unkind, and reprobates are far worse than their reputations.

If you set out to fight the battles of discredited people, don't be too much surprised when they snipe at you from the rear.

Most people sell their souls, and live with a good conscience on the proceeds.

To sell one's soul and not be paid for it, and do the Devil's work without his wages, is perhaps in Heaven's eyes a less flagitious bargain.

It is almost always worth while to be cheated; people's little frauds have an interest which amply repays what they cost us.

When people come and talk to you of their aspirations, before they leave you'd better count your spoons.

All Reformers, however strict their Conscience, live in houses just as big as they can pay for.

People who come downstairs from Ivory Towers splash straight into the gutter.

The tone of people with low aims is always a high one: the talk of those who live purely for the Good is appalling.

People before the public live in the thought of others, and flourish or feel faint as they brighten or dwindle in that mirror.

A virtuous king is a king who has shirked his proper function—to embody for his subjects an ideal of illustrious misbehaviour absolutely beyond their reach.

Some human rôles are so fixed that it is too great a strain to act them in any but the accepted manner. Fathers ought to be tyrannical, and sons ungrateful; grandmothers must demoralize their children's children, and mothers-in-law make all the mischief they can.

Moralists who tell you that Envy is the only vice without a pleasure, have never seen themselves in the eyes of envy.

The Saints see men and women through the haze of their own goodness; and too nice a discrimination of character is a sign that you are not too nice a character yourself.

Only among people who think no evil can Evil monstrously flourish.

Goodness isn't enough; but what delicate glaze it gives to people who are good as well as charming!

Uncultivated minds are not full of wild flowers. Villainous weeds grow in them, and they are the haunt of toads.

How it infuriates a bigot, when he is forced to drag out his dark convictions!

Intolerable to us is the thought that people we detest must be delightful, if delightful people like them.

'Well, for my part,' they say, 'I cannot see the charm of Mrs. Jones.'

'Isn't it just conceivable,' I feel inclined to answer, 'that Mrs. Jones hasn't tried to charm you?'

Charming people live up to the very edge of their charm, and behave as outrageously as the world will let them.

Those who are contemptuous of everyone are more than anyone terrified of contempt.

Never be sorry when fine creatures snap at you; it's a sign that they hunt with another pack.

Don't tell your friends their social faults; they will cure the fault and never forgive you.

Dark and distorting are the minds of people who dislike us; and when we meet them, we make dismal reflections.

I find a fascination, like the fascination for the moth of a star, in those who disdain me.

What a joy to find suddenly among strangers a fish from our little swarm of fishes, a bee from our hive!

We need new friends; some of us are cannibals who have eaten their old friends up: others must have ever-renewed audiences before whom to re-enact the ideal version of their lives.

Don't give to Lovers you will replace, irreplaceable presents.

All our lives we are putting pennies—our most Golden Pennies—into penny-in-the-slot machines that are empty.

We live in a world of monkeys; but often monkeys, at a distance, look like men.

But it is not always easy to treat men and women as apes, and not baboon oneself in the process.

It is a great mistake to talk to one set of people about another set they don't know. We should slink home like cats from our nocturnal outings.

What impossible company we keep in the kind thoughts of those who think kindly of us!

A friend who loved perfection would be the perfect friend, if that love of his didn't shut the door on me.

'But we have the right,' people protest sometimes, 'of entertaining our friends!'
'But have you the right,' we are too polite to answer, 'of forcing us to meet them?'

If we treat people too long with that pretended liking called politeness, we shall find it hard not to like them in the end.

Since few things—as we know—more annoy other people, why do we delight in crabbing their friends?

Those who say everything is pleasant and everyone delightful, come to the awful fate of believing what they say.

How many woes when you marry, how many ancient calamities you invite to the Wedding!

It is a matter of life and death for married people to tell each other's stories; if they didn't, they would burst.

If they lost the incredible conviction that they can change their wives or their husbands, marriage would collapse at once.

The act of flesh is an unsteady basis on which to build the edifice of life.

It is interesting to peep through most keyholes, but not into the bedrooms of married people.

Married women are kept women, and they are beginning to find it out.

Eunuchs are no longer procurable to guard the chastity of females; but there are gentlemen who can be absolutely trusted.

People have a right to be shocked; the mention of unmentionable things is a kind of participation in them.

What are the Queens of Sodom to do when their sons come from school?

Statisticians tell us that in Russia before the First World War six Christs came to save St. Petersburg every year, and were every year seduced by six great ladies of that capital.

What is more disheartening to think of than the unremitting monogamy of grim couples?

How many human types have fallen out of fashion! Where can we find the Black Sheep, the Angel Child, and the Permanent Invalid on her sofa? Into what suburb or sad limbo have departed the dear Old Lady with her cap and laces, the Seducer, the Fop, the Aesthete and the Fallen Daughter?

IV. In the World

People not born on the top of the social tree must have climbed to get there.

The flavour of social success is delicious, though gravely scorned by those to whose lips the cup has not been proffered.

You should wear in the Great World your heart on your sleeve, but it must be a sham one.

The impulse of our nature to people the world with Gods seems pretty in lovers: in Snobs we dislike it.

The hallucinations of sex are not to be trusted, but we can count on our worldly illusions to keep us company to the grave.

And yet to be worldly, to hold to the world's simple creed and believe in its heaven, must surely stagger the faith of the firmest believer.

The spread of Atheism among the young is awful; I give no credit, however, to the report that some of them do not believe in Mammon.

It is the wretchedness of being rich that you have to live with rich people.

Eat with the Rich, but go to the play with the Poor, who are capable of Joy.

You cannot be both fashionable and first-rate.

All worldly goods are good; why otherwise should the world pursue them? And yet the old indictment stands; and garlands and vainglories are best as baubles for our thoughts to play with, like those diadems which drunken Kalenders take and give each other at the doors of Persian wine-shops, a brick beneath their heads, their feet resting on the Seven Stars.

I love money; just to be in the room with a millionaire makes me less forlorn.

Wealthy people should be segregated like lepers to keep them from contaminating others.

To suppose, as we all suppose, that we could be rich and not behave as the rich behave, is like supposing that we could drink all day and stay sober.

Rich people would not so enjoy their little meannesses if they knew how much their friends enjoy them.

Every situation in life provides us ready-made with ways of behaving which perfectly fit it.

Quality-folk are seldom at their ease with Intellectuals; and what a Hell of mischief they make among them!

And when in their azure veins they dip their pens of gold, how vapid, and (but hush!) how vulgar are the books they write!

The ladies who try to keep their Beauty are the ladies who lose it.

There is a toad in every social dish, however well they cook it.

I rather like singing for my supper; what grates on my ears is the song of the other singers.

'I have eaten from the timbrel,' I chant, 'I have drunk from the cymbal, I have carried the sacred vessel, I have crept beneath the bridal chamber.'

More fascinating, at a party, than any other music is the rushing sound of fashionable voices;—the vociferation of all those fairies, each faintly blowing its own trumpet.

There are people whose society I find delicious; but when I sit alone and think of them, I shudder.

Ladies there are who know too much of London, and stand petrified, like Lot's wife, when she looked back on Sodom.

'When people say they hate gossip, remember,' the son of a celebrated upholsterer once warned me, 'that some of them do really hate it.'

There are such astonishing things to be told about men and women, and hardly a man or a woman to whom one dares to tell them.

If you want to be thought a liar, always tell the truth.

To say what you think will certainly damage you in society; but—why should I refrain my mouth?—a free tongue is worth a thousand invitations.

When we find it amusing to shock people, we forget how shocking an experience it is.

Hearts that are delicate and kind and tongues that are neither;—these make the finest company in the world.

Nice men are not nice-minded, but—with a few sublime exceptions—nice women are.

Those who talk on the razor-edge of double-meanings pluck the rarest blooms from the precipice on either side.

How full is the world of Fallen Angels!

Beware of the execrable talk to be heard in certain drawing-rooms of this stony-hearted city. You may find you can't live without it.

How pleasant, with the impunity of years, to sip those cups of enchantment which would have poisoned our youth!

Friendship in the middle-classes is founded on respect; in the world of fashion they simply adore men and women whom not one of them would dream of trusting around the corner.

The fundamental distinction between the good and bad eggs of the world is one which people of the World find convenient to ignore.

The charitable attempt not to smell the smell of a bad egg only makes it worse.

To win a friend is Success; but snatch the friend of a friend, and then blow your trumpet!

We need two kinds of acquaintances, one to complain to, while we boast to the others.

One can be bored until boredom becomes a mystical experience.

When we talk politely of new books with a new acquaintance, what chasms, abysmally, yawn between us!

But what festivals of unanimity we celebrate when we meet what I call a 'Milver'—a fellow-fanatic whose thoughts chime in a sweet ecstasy of execration with our own!

Those who like the same thing find it the hardest thing in the world to hate each other.

'O Joy!' sings a bird in the heart. 'O Joy!' another bird answers; while the world, like a large, thoughtful cat, sits by and watches.

Words aren't always mere words: a few inaudible articulations may fetter two people together for life.

V. Art and Letters

The indefatigable pursuit of an unattainable Perfection,—even though nothing more than the pounding of an old piano,—is what alone gives a meaning to our life on this unavailing Star.

The test of a vocation is the love of the drudgery it involves.

Artists who don't love their art are more numerous, and more unhappy, than we think.

The Muses are vindictive Virgins, who avenge themselves inexorably on those who get tired of their charms.

We should nourish our Souls on the dew of Poesy, and manure them as well.

Slavery and Infamy are the merited chastisements of Success.

Walk in the gutter if you can.

The great art of writing is the art of making people real to themselves with words.

Style is a magic wand; everything it touches turns to gold.

Poets' words have wings: they float up the stairs of palaces on them.

What a Paradise for poets the Great World would be, if any discrimination were made there between fine gold and brass!

Fine writers should split hairs together, and sit side by side, like friendly apes, to pick the fleas from each other's prose.

Authors know that the Age of Miracles is not over; how otherwise explain the transfiguration of asses who praise their writings into exquisite arbiters of taste?

Desperate writers, who once by their cries of agony wrung tears from tender-hearted readers, come to prefer the glittering smiles of hostesses with hearts as hard as their marble mantel-pieces.

A best-seller is the gilded tomb of a mediocre talent.

If you are losing your leisure, look out! You may be losing your soul.

Poverty and her sister Solitude, to whom princely talents used to look for their tuition—how these two shabby Maids of Honour are hooted at now by the young!

Writers who write for money don't write for me.

The notion of making money by popular work, and then retiring to do good work on the proceeds, is the most familiar of all the devil's traps for artists.

What I like in a good author is not what he says, but what he whispers.

Nothing is perfect in this world; and in spite of the noise they make and their big incomes, the complacency of our full-blown authors is not untroubled at odd moments, I am told, by the thought of that little group, just around the corner, of unimportant, unimpressed, jeering, sneering people.

How gay it would be to glitter, with no fellow-performers, alone in the limelight!

Every author, however modest, keeps a most outrageous vanity chained like a madman in the padded cell of his breast.

When we see what people we like will do for money, best it is to be sad and say nothing.

After all, a little good taste does no harm, and the fever of Perfection is not catching.

The most heart-breaking of all people are those who bow with us before our Gods, and then skip off to the shrines of the false ones.

What humbugs we are, who pretend to live for Beauty, and never see the Dawn!

The vitality of a new movement in Art or Letters can be accurately gauged by the fury it arouses.

If you try hard enough to seem to like pictures, you will like them in the end.

What sight in the world is sadder than the sight of a lady we admire admiring a nauseating picture?

If you are up to date today, how dismally out of date you will look tomorrow!

He who goes against the fashion is himself its slave.

All our affirmations are mere matters of chronology; and our bad taste nothing more than the bad taste of the age we live in.

If we're told that an odd piece of our china is worth a hundred pounds,—how rare its beauty!

How amazing are those moments when we unimaginably possess our own possessions!

We who travel thousands of miles to gaze on Beauty, are rather put out by the flaming at home of unfashionable sunsets over fashionable shops.

VI. Myself

The extreme oddness of Existence is what reconciles me to it.

Our personal affairs are not really worthy, as Plato said, of our consideration; the fact that we are forced to take them seriously (as I was forced to run after my hat when it did blow off today), being, as he said, the ignoble part of our condition.

My life is a bubble; but how much solid cash it costs to keep afloat that Bubble!

I like to walk down Bond Street, thinking of all the things I don't desire.

Why should my Soul so rejoice in the crimes placarded by the evening papers, and never weary, in the streets of this cathedral city, of dallying with images of wrong?

'Let me cease,' I pray, 'O thou Perfectly Awakened, to remain as an ape in the great world-forest, perpetually ascending and descending in search of the fruits of folly.'

To count all things as vanity and yet nothing as vain; to wander through the show of things without illusion, or care, or desire, or disappointment; is not this (for why art thou proud, O Dust and Ashes?) the way to walk the London streets?

How Reason totters in her contemplative tower, when people say that they have seen me in the street!

But how hard it is, as Pyrrho of Elis said, to discard our human nature!

I like my universe as immense as possible, grim, pitiless and icy.

When to the lady I met at luncheon I tried to explain that there is no enchantment in life like that of disenchantment with it, she looked at me as if I were a cloud, or a steeple on the horizon, and her answer was as cold as the moon.

When I see those beautiful and mysterious apparitions we call people, I like to think of their adorations one for another; how they love to gaze in the mirrors of each other's eyes.

'O, for an axe!' my soul cries out in railway stations, 'to hew limb from limb all the fiends and Jezebels between me and the ticket-office!'

When I come in talk on a blank wall of stupidity facing me, why do I go and break my bald head against it?

'Isn't it odd,' I said, as we were looking at the roses with those ladies, 'to think that flowers are the reproductive organs of the plants they grow on?'

People who live among photographs of their friends are not friends for me.

I might give my life for my Friend, but he'd better not ask me to do up a parcel.

Like other Moralists, I like to poke about in that dark cabinet, the human heart, and expose its shady corners.

And what pursuit is more elegant than that of collecting the ignominies of our nature and transfixing them, each on the bright pin of a polished phrase?

Aphorisms are salted and not sugared almonds at Reason's feast.

On scenes of worldly splendour I gaze with eyes more mild than those of Moses when, at the sight of the Golden Calf and the dancing, his heart waxed wroth within him.

And the tremendous Enigma which so troubled the soul of King David—the prosperity of the Wicked, and the Righteous as withered grass—this moral paradox does not spoil my appetite in the least.

I like diaphanous illusions, with the shapes of things as they are showing not too faintly through them.

When people tinkle coronets in the conversation I am inordinately solaced.

I don't hate the Aristocracy; but I do wish they wouldn't publish slip-slop with their photographs in the penny papers.

People say that life is the thing, but I prefer reading.

It is the misery of young people that they have to read one another's books.

I hate having new books forced upon me, but how I love cram-throating other people with them!

From the bright, unbookish constellations my thoughts float back to the dim-lit reading-room of this circulating library, the earth.

The world, as I know from my books, is full of abominable evil; even some of these books have never been returned.

Of all the themes of sentimental novels most of all I love a marriage, loveless in appearance, between a high-souled hero and heroine who really do adore each other, but are too proud—ah, far too proud!—to avow it;
Till suddenly,
After years of icily polite relations,
The flame of their mutual ardour blazes out,
And they fall at last
(While I all but swoon away with bliss),
Into the heaven of each other's arms.

I cannot claim to be a dainty feeder; I like to read of frantic passions, and am not at all reluctant to wade ankle-deep in blood.

Amid the mirrored corridors, the fountains and gardens of the Versailles within me, struts his bewigged majesty, my Soul.

I love to take a romantic view of my life, and I hate it.

How often my Soul visits the National Gallery, and how seldom I go there myself!

Just as remorse at feeling no remorse is a form of the holiest contrition, so my coldness, when beauty leaves me cold, I take as the proof of how warmly I love it.

I make no immoderate demands; my hopes for my declining years are not greedy. In January—like an old French unbeliever I have read of—I begin to think of the strawberry season; and I look forward, when that is over, to the ripening of peaches in August.

I shouldn't mind, though, living to my hundredth year, like Fontenelle, who never wept nor laughed, never ran nor interrupted anyone, and never lost his temper; to whom all the science of his day was known, but who all his life adored three things—music, painting and women—about which he said he understood absolutely nothing.

Or like Huet, that gay old Bishop of Avranches ('*flos Episcoporum*' a German scholar called him), who lived to be ninety-one, and read Theocritus every year in his favourite month of May.

Or again I think with envy of the octogenarian Firdausi, who realized the dream he had dreamed in his childhood when, gazing into the canal which flowed by his father's garden, the Persian boy had reflected that it would be a fine thing to leave an image of himself in the world that passes.

Or the learned old Baron Walckenaer, who wrote important books on spiders, solitary bees and Madame de Sévigné; who established on a sound historical basis the chronology of Ninon de Lenclos' lovers, and published a romance called '*l'Ile de Wight*,' in which Island he located his dream of bliss and his ideal habitation.

It would have been a disillusion for the Baron had he known how, standing on a little platform at the top of his house at Farringford, and gazing up through a telescope at the icy constellations which hung in a horror of bottomless space above that island, Tennyson would sometimes shiver, and, for a moment, almost doubt the existence of his benevolent Creator.

But most of all I envy the octogenarian poet who joined three words—
'Go, lovely Rose'—

so happily together, that he left his name to float down through Time on the wings of a phrase and a flower.

When I look at the Ocean, which seemed so inadequate an object of contemplation to Coleridge;—he and Wordsworth were sailing in 1798 on their memorable visit to Germany from Yarmouth in the Hamburg packet, and on Monday, the 17th of September, when the ship was out of sight of land and Coleridge came on deck and gazed at the objectless waters, he was exceedingly disappointed, he tells us, by the narrowness and nearness of the horizon, and was aware of none of that immensity which he had expected to find in such an unimpeded sea-prospect;—so poorly indeed can objects directly before our senses satisfy the Imagination, that 'awful Power,' as his fellow-tourist was afterwards to call it;—when, as I say, I look at the Ocean, I remedy the defect which Coleridge noted by contemplating it through the magnifying glass of our poetic vocabulary; and by calling it 'unpathed,' 'unfathomed,' 'insatiate,' and 'outrageous,' I arrive at a more adequate conception of the view of flat water before me.

There are great youths too, whose achievements one may envy; the boy David who slew Goliath and Bishop Berkeley who annihilated, at the age of twenty-five, in 1710, the external World in an octavo volume; and the young David Hume, who, in 1739, by sweeping away all the props of the human understanding, destroyed for ever the possibility of knowledge.

To be an elegant and acrimonious scholar, and make emendations in Greek texts that shall fill the world with wonder;

Or an illustrious Egyptologist, with spectacles and a white beard;

Or a Lord of Thought, and sum up the universe in a single phrase;

And know all about it, whatever it is, and break the teeth of the young lions, break their great teeth in their mouths;

Or to lie in bed day after day like Joubert, in a pink dressing-gown, trying to think nothing and feel no emotion?

How hard it is for the Good to go wrong! I seem to find all the pleasant paths of Transgression barred and barricaded against me.

Round and round the world, on the storms that blow always about the Southern Pole, albatrosses float for ever; and only once a year do they land to lay their eggs on some Antarctic island of the South Pacific. So from the circumgyrations of its skiey wheelings my soul descends to hatch once in a great while its Meditations.

How I should like to distil my disesteem of my contemporaries into prose so perfect that all of them would have to read it!

But good style depends, the Persian critics tell us, upon freedom from monetary troubles. Only thus, they say, can one arrive at perfect diction.

When by sips of champagne and a few oysters they can no longer keep me from fading away into the infinite azure, 'you cannot,' I shall whisper my faint last message to the world, 'be too fastidious.'

LAST WORDS

LAST WORDS

Growing old is no gradual decline, but a series of tumbles, full of sorrow, from one ledge to another. Yet when we pick ourselves up we find that our bones are not broken; while not unpleasing is the new terrace which lies unexplored before us.

And far below we may pluck from the Tree of Life its mellowest fruit, the joy of Survival, which can only ripen there.

'Yes,' I said one afternoon in the Park, as I looked at the people of Fashion, moving slow and well-dressed in the sunshine, 'but how about the others, the Courtiers and Beauties and Dandies of the past? They wore fine costumes, and glittered for their hour in the summer air. What has become of them?' I somewhat rhetorically asked. They were all dead now. Their day was over. They were cold in their graves.

And I thought of those austere spirits who, in garrets far from the Park and Fashion, had scorned the fumes and tinsel of the loud World.

But, good Heavens! those severe spirits were, it occurred to me, all, as a matter of fact, quite as dead as the others.

If it didn't all depend on me; if I wasn't bound to vin-
dicate the Truth on all occasions, and shout down every
falsehood, standing alone in arms against a sea of Error,
and holding desperately in place the hook from which
Truth and Righteousness and Good Taste hang as by a
thread and tremble over the unspeakable abyss; if but for
a day or two;—it cannot be. I cannot let art and civilization go crashing into chaos. Suppose the skies should fall
in while I was napping and the round world collapse into
stardust again?

'What an intolerable young person!' I exclaimed, the
moment he had left the room. 'How can one sit and listen
to such folly? The arrogance and ignorance of these young
men! And the things they write, and their pictures!'
'It's all pose and self-advertisement I tell you—'
'They've got no reverence!' I gobbled.
Now why on earth do I do it? I know it unhairs my
head and makes my joints rigid;—why then do I go on
talking myself into a toothless old fogey?

Shabby old waistcoat, what made the heart beat that you
used to cover? Funny-shaped hat, where are the hopes that
once nested beneath you? Old shoes, hurrying along what
dim paths of the Past did I wear out your soles?

Oh, dear, this living and eating and growing old; these
doubts and aches in the back, and want of interest in
Nightingales and Roses. . . .

Am I the person who used to wake in the middle of the night and laugh with the joy of living? Who worried about the existence of God, and danced with young ladies till the lark-light? Who sang 'Auld Lang Syne' and howled with sentiment, and more than once gazed at the full moon through a blur of great, romantic tears?

Mind you, I don't say that their eyes aren't bigger than ours, their eyelashes longer, their faces more pink and plump;—and they can skip about with an agility of limb which we cannot equal. But all the same a great deal too much is made of these painted dolls.

Think of the thinness of their conversation!

Depicted in gaudy tints on the covers of paper novels they look well enough; and they make a better appearance, I daresay, in punts. But is that a reason why they should be allowed to disturb the decorum of tables, and interrupt with their anecdotes and giggles our grave consultations?

One Autumn, a good many years ago—I forget the exact date, but it was a considerable time before the 'Great' War —I spent a few weeks in Venice in lodgings that looked out on an old Venetian garden. There was a rustic temple at the end of the garden, and on its pediment stood some naked, shabby, gesticulating statues—heathen Gods and Goddesses I vaguely thought them;—and above, among the yellowing trees, I could see the belfry of a small con-vent—a convent of Nuns vowed to contemplation, *sepolte vive,* who were immured there for life, and never went outside the convent walls.

The belfry was so near that when, towards dusk, the convent bell began to ring against the sky, I could see its bell-rope and clapper moving; and sometimes, as I sat there at my window, I would think about the mysterious existence, so near me, of those life-renouncing virgins.

Very clearly I remember the look of that untidy garden, of those gesticulating statues, and of that convent bell swinging against the sky; but the thoughts that I thought about those Nuns I have completely forgotten. They probably weren't of any especial interest.

It came back to me this rainy afternoon for no reason, the memory of an afternoon long ago alone in the country, when, at the end of an autumn day, I had stood at the rain-dashed window and gazed out at the dim landscape; and as I watched the yellowing leaves blown about the garden, I had seen a flock of birds rise above the half-denuded poplars and wheel in the darkening sky. I had felt there was a mysterious meaning in that moment, and in that flight of dim-seen birds an augury of ill-omen for my life. It was a mood of autumnal, minor-poet melancholy, a mood with which, it had occurred to me, I might stuff out, lugubriously, the rhymes of a sonnet.

But my Sonnet about those birds—those Starlings, or whatever they were—will, I fear, never be written now. For how can I now recapture the sadness, the self-pity of youth?

Alas! What do the compensations of age after all amount to? What joy can the years bring half so sweet as the un-happiness they take away?

How the years pass and life changes, how all things float down the stream of Time and vanish; how friendships fade, and illusions crumble, and hopes dissolve, and piece after solid piece of soap melts away in our hands as we wash them!

Life, I often thought, would be so different if only I had one; but in the meantime I went on fastening scraps of paper together with pins.

Opalescent, infinitely desirable, in the window of a sta-tioner's around the corner, gleamed the vision of my day-dreams. Every day I passed it, but every day my thoughts were distracted by some hope, some disillusion, some meta-physical perplexity, or giant preoccupation with the world's Woe.

And then one morning my pins gave out. I met this crisis with manly resolution; putting my bowler hat on, I went around the corner and bought three paste-pots and took them home. At last the spell was broken. But Oh, at what a cost!

Unnerved and disenchanted, I sat facing those pots of nauseating paste, with nothing now to wait for but death.

Like the Aztec Emperors of ancient Mexico who each year took a solemn oath to make the Sun pursue his wonted journey, I too have vowed to corroborate and help sustain the Solar System; vowed that by no vexed thoughts of mine, no attenuating doubts, nor malicious skepticism, nor hypercritical analysis, shall the great Frame of Things be compromised or shaken.

No one last month but myself seems to have seen it; there was apparently no notice taken of the unwonted, superabundant flourish of the Blackthorn under the black skies of March all over England, when the hedges shone like walls of moonlight in the fields, and all those gnarled little miserly trees showed themselves off in their pale, silvery wealth.

In all our flower-coloured Poesy I find no mention of this aftershadow of the February snow, this foreglimmering of the white splendour of May. Not one of our purblind poets seems ever to have gone afield to gaze at this ghost.

Like the late Dr. Johnson, when at the age of seventy-two he retired to that summer-house at Streatham to plan a life of greater diligence, I too sometimes go off by myself and resolve to spend eight hours of all my remaining days in some grave employment.

But with all that I know about life, all this cynical and sad knowledge of what happens and must happen, all the experience and caution and disillusion stored and packed in the uncanny grey matter of my cerebrum—with all this inside my bald head, how can I ever dream of banging it against the Stars?

How can they say my life isn't a success? Have I not for more than sixty years got enough to eat and escaped being eaten?

The old know what they want; the young are sad and bewildered.

Don't let young people confide in you their aspirations; when they drop them they will drop you.

There is more felicity on the far side of baldness than young men can possibly imagine.

The denunciation of the young is a necessary part of the hygiene of older people, and greatly assists the circulation of their blood.

But what if we can find no freshly-kindled fires for our wet blankets to put out?

To deprive elderly people of their bogeys is as bad as snatching from babies their big stuffed bears.

Moonshine is all moonshine to me.

Thank heavens, the sun has gone in, and I don't have to go out and enjoy it.

Give me a bed and a book and I'm happy.

The mere process of growing old together will make the slightest acquaintance seem a bosom-friend.

What with its crude awakenings can youth know of the rich returns of awareness to elderly people from their after-noon naps; of their ironic thoughts and long retrospections, and the sweetness they taste of not being dead?

When elderly invalids meet with fellow-victims of their own ailments, then at last real conversation begins, and life is delicious.

Because once, unbelievably, in the past, they underwent that amazing mutation, there are elderly people who will tell you that they know what Love is.

The follies we couldn't see through in our youth are what make us play the fool when we are old.

Unrequited affections are in youth unmitigated woes; only later on in life do we learn to appreciate the charm of these bogus heart-breaks.

'Go to the ruins,' whispers the excavated voice of Babylonian disillusion, 'and behold the skulls of the former and the latter; who was the evil-doer, and who the benefactor?'

All my life, as down an abyss without a bottom, I have been pouring van-loads of information into that vacancy of oblivion I call my mind.

Pins, penknives, spectacles, scissors, great paper-cutters, umbrellas, and friends as large as life—the things I lose grow bigger and bigger every day, and one day soon I shall lose the big world itself.

The Universe is becoming a bore.

'Since you're going straight back to Chelsea, would you mind taking these plovers' eggs to poor Gertrude? She's so ill; but she eats plovers' eggs, and these have just come up fresh from Norfolk.'

'Of course, you won't do it,' whispered a voice in my ear, as I carried that little mossy basket of eggs on the Underground; 'You won't do it; you're too white-livered a milksop. But a real Lord of Life with a zest for experience, who wanted to know what it feels like to snap his fingers at decent behaviour, would take those eggs home and eat them himself. But you,' from his realm underground Satan sneered, 'haven't the guts to do it.'

When hope fades away and belief and craving, and we come to contemplate in temporal things only their eternal meanings, then our life ceases at last to be a sham and a failure; and when we die, dainty will be our death.

I got up with Stoic fortitude of mind in the cold this morning; but afterwards, in my hot bath, I joined the school of Epicurus. I was a Materialist at breakfast; after that an Idealist; and as I smoked my first cigarette I transcendentally turned the world to vapour. But when I began to read *The Times* I had no doubt of an externally existing world.

So all the morning and all the afternoon opinions kept flowing into and out of my mind; till by the time the enormous day was over, it had been filled by most of the widely-known Theories of Existence, and emptied of them.

This long speculation of life, this syllogizing that always goes on inside me, this running over and over of hypothesis and surmise and supposition—one day this infinite Argument will have ended, the debate will be for ever over, I shall have come to an indisputable conclusion, and my brain will be at rest.

EPILOGUE

EPILOGUE

'What funny coats you wear, dear Readers! And your
hats! The thought of your hats does make me laugh, and
I think your sex-theories quite horrid.'

Thus across the great gulf of Time I send, with a wave
of my hand, a greeting to that quaint people we call Posterity, whom I, like other great writers, claim as my readers,—urging them to hurry up and get born, that they may
have the pleasure of reading *Trivia*.

> *Quale nei plenilunii sereni*
> *Trivia ride tra le ninfe eterne—*
> IL PARADISO